DUTY
HONOR
COUNTRY

DUTY
HONOR
COUNTRY

MacArthur

A Pictorial
Autobiography

McGraw-Hill Book Company
New York
Toronto
London

Duty—honor—country.
Those three hallowed words reverently dictate
what you ought to be,
what you can be,
what you will be.

—Douglas MacArthur
Sylvanus Thayer Speech
West Point, May 12, 1962

PICTURE CREDITS

Pictorial Parade: 4; 32; 49; 74, bottom left; 97; 128, top; Black Star: 218; Fred Ward, Black Star, 44, bottom; Owen, Black Star, 78, top.   Culver: 91, bottom; 128, bottom left.   Will Weissberg: 207, middle left; 211, top.   U.S. Marine Corps Photo: 80, bottom.   U.S. Navy Photo: 81, right bottom 82; 90, bottom right and left; 149, top.   Underwood & Underwood: 92, bottom; 114, top, and bottom right; 149, bottom; 154-155; 168-169, top; 171, bottom; 201.   Pix, Inc.: 101, top; 108, bottom; Carl Bakal—Pix, Inc., 120, top, and 126; Fred Sparks—Pix, Inc., 129, top left.   FPG: 56-57; 84-85; 91, top; 94-95; 103, top; 136-137, top; 142; 150, bottom left; 162; 171, top; 183.   Paris Match: 16; 17; 18; 19; 21; 46, top left; 80, top left; 102, top; 118-119; 201; 214, top left and top center.   United Press International: 45, bottom; 96, top; 102, bottom; 176-177, bottom; 153, 196, bottom; 204, 207, bottom left; 209, middle right; 214, bottom; 216, top. Department of the Army: 54; 80, middle; 81, top and right top; 83, bottom; 86-87; 92, top; 99, top; 103, bottom; 104, bottom; 106-107; 108, top; 150, top and bottom right; 158, top and bottom; 167, top; 169, bottom; 180, bottom left; 207, middle right. 206, top.   Mrs. Douglas MacArthur Collection: i-vi; 11; 12; 23; 52, bottom left and bottom right; 66, bottom; 74, top, and bottom right; 75, bottom; 110-111; 124; 125; 128, bottom right; 129, bottom; 135; 160, top; 185; 204-205, top and bottom; 209, bottom; 211, bottom; 212, top, bottom left and center.   Wide World: 1-2; 8; 9; 20, bottom; 22, top; 24-25; 31, bottom; 33; 34, bottom left and right; 35, top; 36, top and bottom; 37; 39; 38; 41; 42-43; 44, top; 46, bottom and top right; 47; 50-51; 52, top; 62-63; 65; 66, top; 72, top; 73; 75, top; 76, top right and bottom left; 79, bottom; 80, top right; 83, top; 90, top; 99, bottom; 100, bottom; 114, bottom left; 120, bottom left; 122; 129, top right; 130; 137, bottom; 160, bottom right; 167, bottom; 176-177, top; 180, bottom right and top; 194; 205; 201; 202, top left and right; 206, bottom; 207, top and bottom right; 209, middle left; 212, bottom right; 214, top right; 216, top and bottom.   Brown Brothers: 5, top and bottom; 6-7; 10; 14; 20, top; 22, bottom left and right; 31, top; 34, top; 35, bottom; 45, top; 48, bottom and top; 64; 68-69; 70; 76, bottom right; 78, bottom; 79, top; 88; 96, bottom; 100, top; 101, bottom; 109; 120, bottom right; 131; 140, top and bottom; 139; 160, bottom left; 165; 196, top; 202, bottom; 209, top.

DUTY—HONOR—COUNTRY

Library of Congress Catalog
Card Number: 65-25518

44304

FIRST EDITION

Contents

Part I

Education of a General

Heir of the Scottish clan MacArtair, grandson of a distinguished justice of the Supreme Court of the District of Columbia, and son of a hero of the Civil War, Douglas MacArthur was born in 1880 at the Arsenal Branch in Little Rock, Arkansas.

Educated to the demands of personal sacrifice, of duty and loyalty to one's country, he spent his early years in the vivid and exciting life of the western frontier. In 1898, during the war with Spain, his father was appointed to the rank of brigadier general and assigned to duty in the Philippine Islands. Under his stewardship the first foundations of civil administration and economic development were realized. The sons of the same Filipinos who fought his father so tenaciously were to help Douglas gain his greatest fame.

On June 13, 1899,

I enrolled at the United States Military Academy. Life at West Point is rigid discipline in an atmosphere of culture and learning. But all is not drudgery in this world apart from all other worlds. There was the thrill of high competition on the athletic field, the dances and excitement and gay hours with beautiful ladies. I worked hard and I played hard. There are some incidents of my happy four years there I still recall. One nearly ended my career as a cadet.

Conditions in those days were different from today. Much of the discipline of new cadets was left in the hands of the upper classes. Hazing was practiced with a worthy goal, but with methods that were violent and uncontrolled. President McKinley at Congress' insistence ordered a special court of inquiry which convened in December 1900 to investigate both an incident of alleged hazing, which had occurred a year prior to my entrance, and also the extent to which plebes were subject to hazing. I was summoned to appear before the court as a principal witness in a case

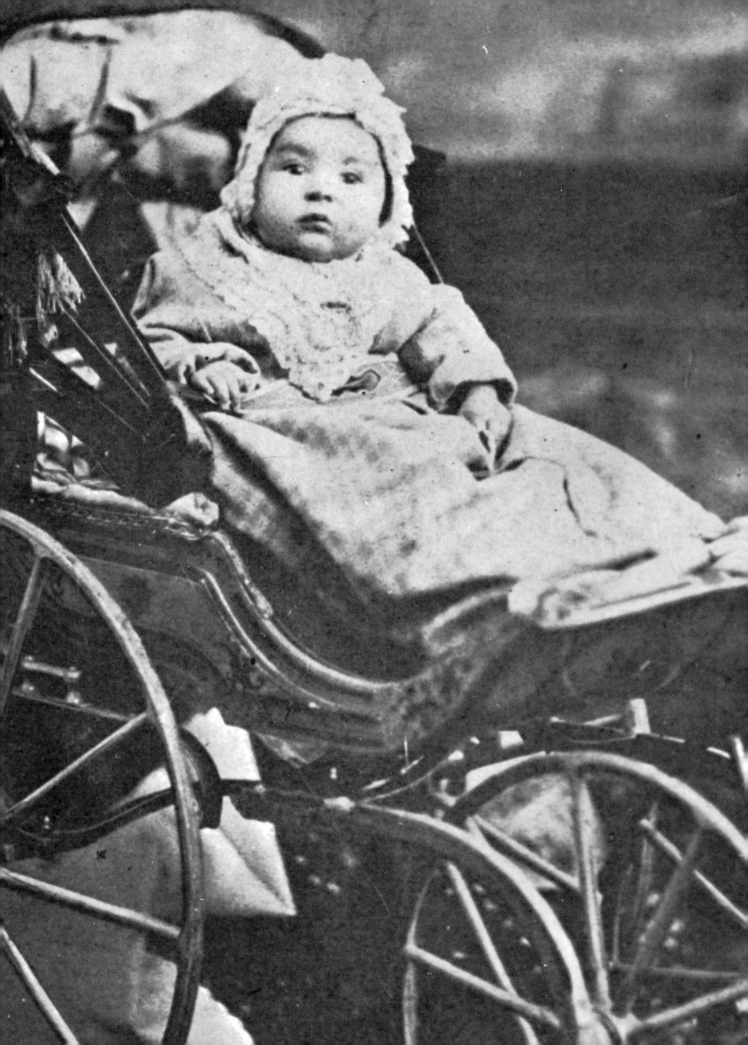

Above:
Lieutenant
General Arthur MacArthur.

Facing page:
At six months.

Below:
Mary Pinkney Hardy,
the General's mother.

in which I had been the so-called victim.

Under questioning I fully explained all the circumstances, but refused to divulge the names of the upper classmen involved. My father and mother had taught me those two immutable principles—never to lie, never to tattle. But here was a desperate situation for me. If the court insisted and ordered me to reveal the names, and I refused to obey the order, it would in all likelihood mean my dismissal and the end of all my hopes and dreams. It would be so easy and expedient to yield, to tell, and who would blame me?

My mother, who was at West Point at the time, sensed the struggle raging in my soul and sent me this message during a recess of the court:

Do you know that your soul is of my soul such a part
That you seem to be fiber and core of my heart?
None other can pain me as you, son, can do;
None other can please me or praise me as you.
Remember the world will be quick with its blame
If shadow or shame ever darken your name.
Like mother, like son, is saying so true
The world will judge largely of mother by you.
Be this then your task, if task it shall be
To force this proud world to do homage to me.
Be sure it will say, when its verdict you've won
She reaps as she sowed: "This man is her son!"

I knew then what to do. Come what may, I would be no tattletale.

Although more than sixty years have come and gone since then, I can still feel the beads of sweat on my brow, still feel my knees giving way under me and that dreadful nausea that I had felt once before when I faced my competitive examination at the city hall in Milwaukee. I did my best to fend off the question, to dodge the issue, but I was no match for the shrewd old heads who sat in judgment. And then the order came, short, peremptory, unequivocal. At the end I grew weak and pleaded for mercy: that my whole life's hope lay in being an officer; that always I had been with the colors; that my father, then on the battle-line 10,000 miles away, was their comrade-in-arms of the Civil and Indian wars; that I would do anything in the way of punishment, but not to strip me of my uniform. And then—I could not go on—I heard the old soldier who presided say, "Court is recessed. Take him to his quarters."

For hours I waited for that dread step of the adjutant coming to put me in arrest. But it never came. The names were obtained through other means. And never again was I to be in doubt about doing what I thought to be right, never again were my knees to knock in trepidation as to my fate, only once again was the old nausea to strike.

Those four years at West Point held so much of those glories of youth that mean so little in the lexicon of later life. I remember the first baseball game ever to be played with the midshipmen of the Naval Academy at Annapolis on May 18, 1901. I was in left field for the cadets, with the Navy stands right next to me. It was a period of great prominence for my father as governor general of the Philippines. It was an overcast day and the Middies carried raincoats. I shall never forget the blast that razzed me when the Army took the field. Every raincoat was swinging, every Navy voice joining the ribald ditty:

> "Are you the Governor General
>   Or a hobo?
> Who is the boss of this show?
> Is it you or Emilio Aguinaldo?"

But I squared it up. With two out and the score tied at three-all, I worked the Navy pitcher for a base on balls. The umpire had been more than generous to me and the Navy catcher was, to put it mildly, understandingly upset by the call. I was no Ty Cobb, but in those days I could run. I went down on the first pitch and, sure enough, the catcher threw wild, allowing me to go on to third. The throw from the outfield went over the third baseman's head, and I trotted home with what proved to be the winning run in a 4–3 contest. They are fine sportsmen, those Navy files, and when the game was over they treated me as though I really were the governor general. I was far from a brilliant ballplayer, even by the limited standards of college baseball, but that game will always stand out as one of my happiest memories.

And that awful moment when a tactical officer caught me on Flirtation Walk publicly kissing a girl, and instead of reporting me for unbecoming conduct, just grinned and said, "Congratulations, Mister MacArthur."

And the day we went to the horseshow in New York, when my roommate, Charles Severson, and "Dotty" Laurson, the Cadet Captain of "E" Company, and myself slipped away and swaggered into Rector's on Broadway, shook hands with "Diamond Jim" Brady, and called for nine martinis. The astounded bartender asked, "Where are the other six?" and "Dotty," striking a Napoleonic posture, bellowed out, pointing to the six waiting glasses, "Their spirits are here." And then

West Division High School
in Milwaukee where MacArthur prepared
for his West Point examinations.
"The night before the examination,
for the first time
in my life
I could not sleep."

Above:
Graduation, West Point 1903.
(MacArthur second from right)
"Those four years at West Point
held so much of those glories
of youth that mean so little
in the lexicon of later life."

Facing page:
The football team
of West Texas Military Academy.
MacArthur (foreground with
numerals) played end.
1896.

Cadet Douglas MacArthur,
West Point.

we swanked out to a burlesque show. We loved it!

I won my "A," became First Captain of the Corps, and to my amazement recorded the highest scholastic record in twenty-five years. This rating has always astonished me and I have never understood it. There were a number of my classmates who were smarter than I, and I am sure there were even a greater number in the preceding twenty-four classes. I studied no longer nor harder than others, and can only account for such a result by my having, perhaps, a somewhat clearer perspective of events—a better realization that first things come first.

I graduated on June 11, 1903, as a second lieutenant of Engineers with the words of Secretary of War Elihu Root, ringing in my ears: "Before you leave the Army, according to all precedents in our history, you will be engaged in another war. It is bound to come, and will come. Prepare your country for that war."

Early in October, 1904,

I was ordered to join my father in Japan, where he had been sent to observe the Russo-Japanese War. The purpose of our observations was to measure the strength of the Japanese Army and its methods of warfare. In Washington there was a growing uneasiness. In January 1905, President Roosevelt wrote, "If Japan is careful, and is guided by the best minds in her Empire, she can become one of the leaders of the family of great nations; but if she is narrow and insular, if she tries to gain from her victory in the Russo-Japanese War more than she ought to have, she will array against her all the great powers, and however determined she may be she cannot successfully face an allied world." And two months later he addressed the Chairman of the House Committee on Military Affairs, Representative J. A. T. Hull, as follows: "It may be that the Japanese have designs on the Philippines. I hope not. I am inclined to believe not. But I believe we should put our naval and military preparations in such shape that we can hold the Philippines against any foe."

I met all the great Japanese commanders: Oyama, Kuroki, Nogi, and the brilliant Admiral Heihachiro Togo—those grim, taciturn, aloof men of iron character and unshakeable purpose. It was here that I first encountered the boldness and courage of the Nipponese soldier. His almost fa-

1905.
With the Duke of Windsor.

natical belief in and reverence for his Emperor impressed me indelibly.

Nothing illustrates this devotion better than the following incident. The Second Japanese Army under General Yasukata Oku was afflicted by the dread disease of beriberi. The surgeon prescribed a prophylactic put up in a small tin can with the inscription, "To prevent beriberi take one pill three times a day." Soldiers are much the same throughout the world: they took the pill once, spat it out, then dumped the can into the mud. The surgeon was at his wits' end until some bright young officer suggested that the cans be marked, "To prevent beriberi, *the Emperor desires you* to take one pill three times a day." The result was instantaneous. Not a pill was wasted. Nothing but death itself could stop the soldiers from taking the medicine.

I asked one of their signal officers what type of codes were used in transmitting their operational messages. Typically, he was evasive, but later, over a bowl of *sake*, he laughingly confided to me that the most secret messages were sent without dilution in the Japanese language. No foreigner, he said, could understand it.

I was deeply impressed by and filled with admiration for the thrift, courtesy, and friendliness of the ordinary citizen. They seemed to have discovered the dignity of labor, the fact that a man is happier and more contented when constructing than when merely idling away time. But I had the uneasy feeling that the haughty, feudalistic samurai who were their leaders, were, through their victories, planting the seed of eventual Japanese conquest of the Orient. Having conquered Korea and Formosa, it was more than evident that they would eventually strike for control of the Pacific and domination of the Far East.

The reports my father submitted to Washington from Japan went beyond battle tactics and strategy. He was aware that Japanese victory over Russia did not mean Russia's elimination from the Far East. This vast, complex area, restless under the boot of European domination, might well be the arena of future world struggle. As a result, he was ordered to extend his comprehensive evaluations to the colonial lands of the Orient, Southeast Asia, and India. His itinerary would take him from Yokohama to Calcutta, by way of Hong Kong, Singapore, and Rangoon. From Calcutta, he would investigate the Northwest Frontier at Peshwar and Quetta, thence to Bombay, Hyderabad, Bangalore, Madras, and Colombo. He was then to return north through Java, Siam, and Indo-China to Shanghai. Several months were to be devoted to China. I was to accompany him as an aide-de-camp.

We were nine months in travel, traversing countless miles of lands so rich in color, so fabled in legend, so vital to history that the experience was without doubt the most important factor of preparation in my entire life. We discussed defense plans behind closed doors and inspected military fortifications and critical areas on the spot. We sat in the charmed circles of the chancelleries of the strong and the weak. Kings and viceroys and high commissioners lay bare their hopes and fears. We listened to both sides of the famous Curzon-Kitchener feud—that age-old struggle between the civil and the military to fix the exact line of demarcation between executive control and the professional duty of the soldier. We traversed the path to Afghanistan with the "King of the Khyber," Sir Bindon Blood; we rode the Grand Trunk Road of Kipling's *Kim;* we reached out from Darjeeling in trace of Sir Francis Younghusband's penetration of Tibet in search of the Grand Llama. We saw the strength and the weakness of the colonial system, how it brought law and order, but failed to develop the masses along the essential lines of education and political economy. We rubbed elbows with millions of the underprivileged who knew nothing of the difference between the system of the free world and the slave world, but were interested only in getting a little more food in their stomachs, a little better coat on their backs, a little stronger roof over their heads.

The true historic significance and the sense of destiny that these lands of the western Pacific and Indian Ocean now assumed became part of me. They were to color and influence all the days of my life. Here lived almost half the population of the world, with probably more than half of the raw products to sustain future generations. Here was western civilization's last earth frontier. It was crystal clear to me that the future and, indeed, the very existence of America, were irrevocably entwined with Asia and its island outposts. It was to be sixteen years before I returned to the Far East, but always was its mystic hold upon me.

Despite President Wilson's attempts at maintaining neutrality, the sinking of the Lusitania *precipitated America's entry in World War I. After*

Lieutenant General MacArthur at High Point, Virginia.

heroic service in Vera Cruz and promotion to the General Staff in Washington, MacArthur suggested the formation of a division to be formed from all of the states in the union—The Rainbow Division.

During August, 1917,

the 42nd Division was assembled at Camp Mills near Garden City on Long Island, New York, with Major General William A. Mann as commander and myself as chief of staff. The roll of its components listed twenty-six states: infantrymen from New York, Ohio, Iowa, and Alabama; artillerymen from Illinois, Indiana, and Minnesota; engineers from South Carolina, California, and North Carolina; machine-gunners from Pennsylvania, Wisconsin, and Georgia; trench mortarmen from Maryland; military police from Virginia; signalmen from Missouri; ammunition men from Kansas; supply trainmen from Texas; ambulance and field hospital men from New Jersey, Tennessee, Oklahoma, Michigan, Oregon, Nebraska, Colorado, and the District of Columbia; and cavalrymen from Louisiana.

The caliber of both officers and men was excellent. From their ranks came many of the great names that enrich the tablets of military fame. Weapons in modern warfare are a vital factor, but of even greater importance is the human element—the troops who fight the battles, and the personnel who supply, transport, feed, house, and doctor them. In the Rainbow Division the human equation was strikingly expressed by the splendid relationship that existed between the officers and enlisted men, and in the comradeship between the men themselves—a relationship which may have been matched in other military organizations, but certainly was never surpassed. From the division commander down to the private, there was that mutual respect and understanding which made for the accomplishment of objectives. The outfit soon took on a color, a dash, a unique flavor that is the essence of that elusive and deathless thing called soldiering. It has always held a special place in my affection, and to this day I feel a thrill whenever I see the Rainbow's colorful patch.

On July 25th, [1917] in a black, drizzling night, the division unloaded from its buses in front of Château Thierry to relieve the units of the exhausted 26th Division. The Germans were pulling back, and our orders were to press him. Instead of

Promotion to
the General Staff.

a swift retreat, covered by small rearguards, the German tactic was to position troops on rugged slopes and in protecting woods for a desperate defense. They massed machine guns and mortars behind rugged stone walls and in scattered farm buildings. Our artillery was not in sufficient strength to silence this death blaze of Germany. Death beckoned the bravest and the strongest in the deceptive fields of that bright green countryside. It was to be six of the bitterest days and nights of the war for the Rainbow.

We reverted to tactics I had seen so often in the Indian wars of my frontier days. Crawling forward in twos and threes against each stubborn nest of enemy guns, we closed in with the bayonet and the hand grenade. It was savage and there was no quarter asked or given. It seemed to be endless. Bitterly, brutally, the action seesawed back and forth. A point would be taken, and then would come a sudden fire from some unsuspected direction and the deadly counterattack. Positions changed hands time and again. There was neither rest nor mercy.

Step by step, we fought forward: La Croix Rouge Ferme Beauvardes, Forêt de Fère, Villers-sur-Fère. Kilometer by kilometer, we reached the south bank of the Ourcq River. Across the river on the north bank was the enemy's main line of resistance: Meurcy Ferme on his right flank, Sergy his left, Seringes his center. We forced a passage the evening of July 28th, and took Meurcy Ferme in a hand-to-hand fight. I borrowed two battalions from the 4th Division, which was coming up in reserve, and with their help we stormed Sergy at bayonet point, but were thrown out almost immediately. Eleven times it changed hands before we finally held its smoking ruins. The center at Seringes still held. It looked like a small Gibraltar, with its flanking guns and its barricaded streets and houses swarming with troops. I formed our infantry on the south bank of the stream and rushed the town. Their artillery concentrated, their machine guns east and west of the town raked us fore and aft, but nothing could stop the impetus of that mad charge. We forded the river. We ascended the slopes. We seized Hill 184. We killed the garrison in the town to a man. At dusk on July 29th we were in sole possession.

Shortly after midnight, while reconnoitering in front of our outposts, I thought I could hear unusual sounds from the German lines—explosions, the rumbling of many vehicles on the move. Certain the German was withdrawing, I determined to move in on him at once. If I pressed him close enough, he would be unable to reform his line of battle until he reached the Vesle River, many kilometers away. He would have to abandon his piled-up supply dumps. It could not but save us many thousands of precious lives. There was no time to consult division or corps headquarters. I had to rely upon my own judgment and assume all responsibility.

Our front was about 4 kilometers in length. I decided to traverse this line and direct each regiment to move out with one battalion in line of battle, followed by a second in support, and the third in column as reserve. All were to move out simultaneously so that the whole would present an integrated front. I sent a message to the artillery to at once "advance with audacity."

It was 3:30 that morning when I started from our right at Sergy. Taking runners from each outpost liaison group to the next, moving by way of what had been No Man's Land, I will never forget that trip. The dead were so thick in spots we tumbled over them. There must have been at least 2,000 of those sprawled bodies. I identified the insignia of six of the best German divisions. The stench was suffocating. Not a tree was standing. The moans and cries of wounded men sounded everywhere. Sniper bullets sung like the buzzing of a hive of angry bees. An occasional shellburst always drew an angry oath from my guide. I counted almost a hundred disabled guns of various size and several times that number of abandoned machine guns.

Suddenly a flare lit up the area for a fraction of a minute and we hit the dirt, hard. Just ahead of us stood three Germans—a lieutenant pointing with outstretched arm, a sergeant crouched over a machine gun, a corporal feeding a bandolier of cartridges to the weapon. I held my breath waiting for the burst, but there was nothing. The seconds clicked by, but still nothing. We waited until we could wait no longer. My guide shifted his poised grenade to the other hand and reached for his flashlight. They had not moved. They were never to move. They were dead, all dead—the lieutenant with shrapnel through his heart, the sergeant with his belly blown into his back, the corporal with his spine where his head should have been. We left them there, just as they were, gallant men dead in the service of their country.

When I reached our flank regiment just before dawn, I found Colonel Frank McCoy and the gallant chaplain, Father Duffy, just returned from

burying Sergeant Joyce Kilmer under the stump of one of those trees he had immortalized.

On October 1st, the division was moving toward the vast shifting battlefield along the 80-mile front of the Meuse-Argonne. A million American soldiers were to attempt a breakthrough in the center of the Western Front to Sedan, a breakthrough which would mean the collapse of the powerful Hindenburg Line and the defeat of Germany. We slipped and slithered over the battered highways and roads, through dripping patches of forest and by stricken villages and farms. At Montfaucon we were held for several days in its soaked and crowded woods, as a reserve for the 79th Division. I watched its frontal and unsuccessful attack from the old churchyard on the hill. Without warning, a squadron of German planes dived out of nowhere and shot down every one of the dozen or more observation balloons the Army had in the air. In leaving, they flew not a hundred feet above me and I recognized the flowing yellow scarfs of the Richthofen Squadron—the famous "flying circus" created by the German ace, Manfred Baron Von Richthofen.

In 1914, when the great German armies first marched to conquest, they had come through the Argonne, seized it, and had never been dislodged. The terrain was so difficult, so easily defended, that the French had never attempted to attack. It was so powerfully fortified over four years that doubt existed in Allied high circles that any troops in the world could drive out the Germans. The Germans, themselves, boasted they would drown an American attack in its own blood.

Into this red inferno the Americans had jumped off on September 26th, and foot by foot, over scarred and wooded hill and valley, had fought their bloody way from trench to trench to the enemy's main line of resistance. The Germans, alive to the threat, had a machine gun nest behind every rock, a cannon behind every natural embrasure. Here was the key sector of the famous Hindenburg Line, known as the *Krunhilde Stalling*. Here was the last line of the mighty German defenses in the Argonne. Breach it and there would be laid bare Sedan and Mezieres, the two huge German rail centers, through which all the German armies as far away as the North Sea at Ostend were supplied. Take Sedan and every German army to the west would be outflanked. The railroads by which they could withdraw such large masses of troops would be either in American hands or under fire from American guns. It would

Above, facing page
and following pages:
World War I. France. "In the Rainbow Division the human equation was strikingly expressed by the splendid relationship that existed between the officers and enlisted men. The outfit soon took on a color, a dash, a unique flavor that is the essence of that illusive and deathless thing called soldiering."

Above and facing page:
World War I. France.

mean the capture of troops running into the hundreds of thousands. It would mean the end of the war.

Our troops had paid a fearful price in their advance, and particularly at the group of hills known as the Côte-de-Châtillon, the pivot of the entire *Krunhilde Stalling*. Our hard-hitting 32nd Division had ploughed bravely forward only to fall back bleeding and decimated. The 91st Division suffered the same fate. And the famous 1st Division, the Big Red, pride of the Regulars, had bled itself white before the deep trenches, endless wire, and innumerable cannon and machine guns. The Rainbow was brought in to relieve the 1st Division, which had driven a deep salient into the German lines. This salient was dominated by the Côte-de-Châtillon stronghold which raked the Allied flank and thus stopped the advancing line of the American attack. Every effort to go forward had been stopped cold by this flanking fire.

I carefully reconnoitered the desolate and forbidding terrain that confronted my brigade. There were rolling hills, heavily wooded valleys of death between the endless folds of ridges. Puffs of gas and shellfire broke like squalls of wind. I saw at once that the previous advances had failed because it had not been recognized that the Côte-de-Châtillon was the keystone of the whole German position; that until it was captured we would be unable to advance. I proposed to capture the Côte-de-Châtillon by concentrating troops on it, instead of continuing to spread the troops along a demonstratedly unsuccessful line of attack. Both the division and corps commanders approved.

The night of October 11th was wet and black, and I had just completed plans for the attack when Major General Charles P. Summerall, the V Corps commander, entered the candle-lit C.P. He was tired and worn, and I made him drink a cup of steaming black coffee, strong enough to blister the throat.

"Give me Châtillon, MacArthur," he suddenly said, his voice strained and harsh. "Give me Châtillon, or a list of five thousand casualties." His abruptness startled me.

While making a further reconnaissance, I was wounded, but not incapacitated, and was able to continue functioning. I discovered that, as usual, while the German center, where the 1st Division had spent its blood, seemed impregnable, the flanks were vulnerable. His deep belt of wire entanglement and trench dribbled out at the ends. There was where I planned to strike with my

World War I. France.

Training with the Rainbow Division.
Left: Major General William A. Mann,
commander, Colonel Douglas MacArthur,
Chief of Staff.

Alabama cotton-growers on the left, my Iowa farmers on the right. I planned to use every machine gun and every artillery piece as covering fire.

We moved out in the misty dawn, and from then on little units of our men crawled and sneaked and side-slipped forward from one bit of cover to another. When the chance came we would close in suddenly to form squads or platoons for a swift envelopment that would gain a toehold on some slope or deadly hillock. Death, cold and remorseless, whistled and sung its way through our ranks, but by nightfall Hill 288 was in Iowa hands. That night I readjusted and reorganized, and the following day we fought up Hill 282, a frowning height of 900 feet, and fought around and skirted Hill 205 to take the Tuilieres Ferme.

The last defenses of the Côte-de-Châtillon were still before us, but as dusk was falling the First Battalion of the 168th under Major Lloyd Ross moved from the right, while a battalion of the 167th under Major Ravee Norris stalked stealthily from the left toward the gap in the wire. The two battalions, like the arms of a relentless pincer, closed in from both sides. Officers fell and sergeants leaped to the command. Companies dwindled to platoons and corporals took over. At the end, Major Ross had only 300 men and 6 officers left out of 1,450 men and 25 officers. That is the way the Côte-de-Châtillon fell, and that is the way those gallant citizen-soldiers, so far from home, won the approach to final victory.

Facing page,
top and bottom left:
World War I. France.

Facing page, bottom right:
World War I.
Receiving the Distinguished
Service Medal
from General Pershing.

Left:
France.

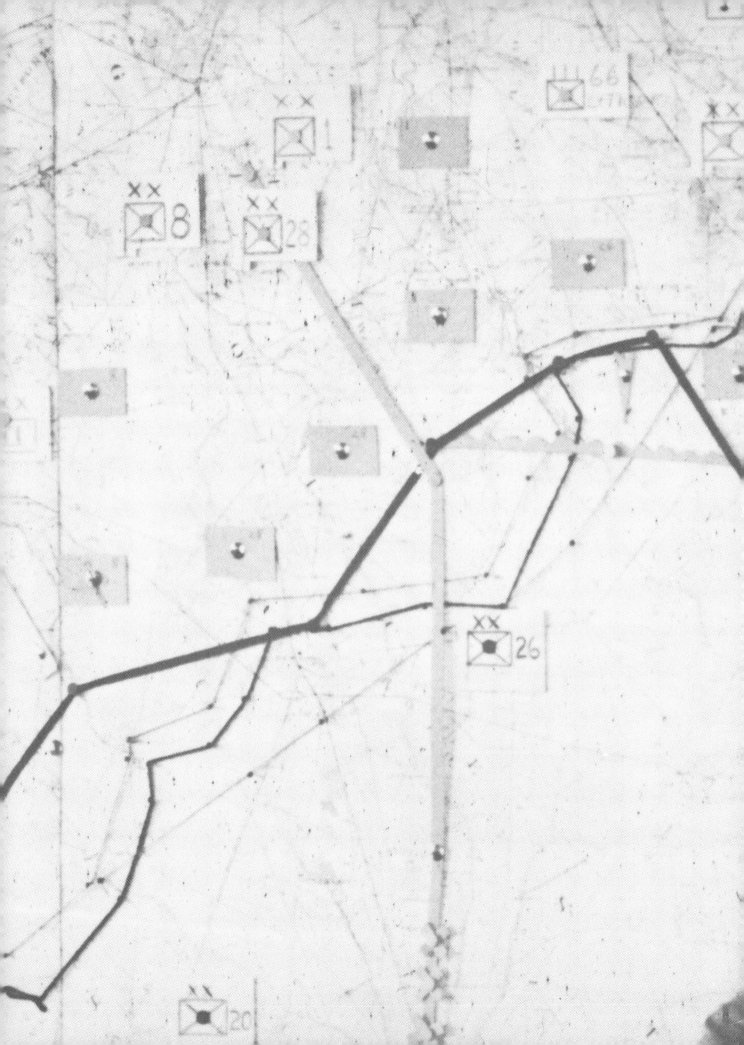

Part II

In Defense of Peace

On June 12, 1919,

I assumed the command at West Point. The entire institution was in a state of disorder and confusion. Due to wartime demands for officers, the normal four-year course had been shortened to one year. The necessity was pressing for creating a new generation of officers for the coming army, as 9,119 had been killed in action or wounded in France.

"West Point is forty years behind the times," General Peyton March, the Chief of Staff, said flatly, on giving me the assignment. Even the proud spirit of the Academy had flagged. In every way, West Point would have to be revitalized, the curriculum re-established.

The atmosphere of public opinion in the United States at that time was not propitious for such an enterprise. It is a singular habit in this country to raise high the military when war threatens, but to ignore security needs in the pleasanter times of peace. If, said many, this was the war to end wars, the war to save democracy for all time, why go on training, at great expense, officers who would never have to fight? Why have a West Point at all? The thing to do is to abolish West Point and install reserve officer training schools at the colleges—in the remote chance that this war might not be the last war, after all.

Congress, too, was in an economic mood and threatened to strip the school to a skeleton. "Back to normalcy" became the slogan of those who professed to be shocked at what they claimed to be the frightful waste of money for war preparation. "Never again," they protested: "economy."

My first move was to go to Washington and contact the leaders in Congress, many of whom I had known previously. Many people in this free country of ours constantly criticize this great body for every woe and trouble that assails them, but I had always found its members patient, courteous, and efficient. When the true facts had been presented to them, they had always acted with patriotic courage and fearless determination, irrespective of party affiliation. And so it was in this case.

I explained:

The government's expenditures for military needs are a form of national insurance from which come dividends year by year. Premiums must be paid to correspond with the needs of our country in peace or in war. A comparatively small outlay by the United States will serve in future to lessen the tremendous expense and the loss of blood for which no money can repay when the unforeseen tragedy is upon us. West Point, together with the United States Naval Academy, represents the apotheosis of the public school system, and in its development there should be that spirit of generous foresight that has marked the educational systems of the nation for the past century.

Congress had passed a compromise bill fixing a three-year course, and later accepted my recommendation to return to a four-year course.

But the greatest problems I found were internal ones. My first report sets them forth as follows:

My assumption of the command of the United States Military Academy synchronized with the ending of an epoch in the life of this institution. With the termination of the World's War the mission of West Point at once became the preparation of officer personnel for the next possible future war. The methods of training here have always been largely influenced by the purpose of producing the type of officer which the Army at large dictated. The excellence with which the Academy's mission has been carried out in the past has been testified on the battlefields of the world for a hundred years and more. The problem which faced the authorities was, therefore, this: Have new conditions developed, have the lessons of the World War indicated that a changed type of officer was necessary in order to produce the maximum of efficiency in the handling of men at arms? West Point, existing solely as a source of supply and a feeder to the Army, if a new era faces the latter, must of necessity train its personnel accordingly.

In meeting this problem those who were charged with the solution undertook the task with a full realization of its seriousness. It was well understood that it was no light affair to attempt even in moderate degree to modify a status which had proved itself so splendidly for a century and more. It was understood that change under the guise of reconstruction was destructive unless clearly and beyond question it introduced something of added benefit. It was recognized that reform to be effective must be evolutionary, and not revolutionary. It was evident that many sources of help, in the nature of advice and consultation, lay outside of the Military Academy in the persons of distinguished officers of the Army at large and of professional educators throughout the country.

Careful analysis yielded the following conclusions: Until the World War, armed conflicts between nations had been fought by a comparatively small fraction of the population involved. These professional armies were composed very largely of elements which frequently required the most rigid methods of training, the severest forms of discipline, to weld them into a flexible weapon for use on the battlefield. Officers were, therefore, developed to handle a more or less recalcitrant element along definite and simple lines, and a fixed psychology resulted. Early in the World War it was realized to the astonishment of both sides that the professional armies, upon which they had relied, were unable to bring the combat to a definite decision. It became evident, due largely to the elaborate and rapid methods of communication and transportation which had grown up in the past generation, that national communities had become so intimate, that war was a condition which involved the efforts of every man, woman and child in the countries affected. War had become a phenomenon which truly involved the nation in arms. Personnel was of necessity improvised, both at the front and at the rear; the magnitude of the effort, both of supply and of combat, was so great, that individuals were utilized with the minimum of training. In general result, this was largely off-set by the high personal type of those engaged. Discipline no longer required extreme methods. Men generally needed only to be told what to do, rather than be forced by the fear of consequence of failure. The great numbers involved made it impossible to apply the old rigid methods which had been so successful when battlelines were not so extensive. The rule of this war can but apply to that of the future. Improvisation will be the watchword. Such changed conditions will require a modification in type of the officer, a type possessing all of the cardinal military virtues as of yore, but possessing an intimate understanding of his fellows, a comprehensive grasp of world and national affairs, and a liberalization of conception which amounts to a change in his psychology of command. This standard became the basis of the construction of the new West Point in the spirit of Old West Point.

To hold fast to those policies typified in the motto of the Academy, "Duty, Honor, Country," to cling to thoroughness as to a lodestar, to continue to inculcate the habit of industry, to implant as of old the gospel of cleanliness—to be clean, to live clean, and to think clean—and yet to introduce a new atmosphere of liberalization in doing away with provincialism, a substitute of subjective for objective discipline, a progressive increase of cadet responsibility tending to develop initiative and force of character rather than automatic performance of stereotyped functions, to broaden the curriculum so as to be abreast of the best modern thought on education, to bring West Point into a new and closer relationship with the Army at large, has been the aim and purpose of my administration.

But it was one thing to say what was wanted and quite another to do it. General March had not exaggerated. Conditions with respect to the course of study were chaotic. Under the stress of war, the educational qualifications for admission had been drastically lowered. The morale of the cadet body was low.

The traditional disciplinary system, so largely built around the prestige and influence of the upper classmen was impossible in a situation where there were no upper classmen. Cadet officers had never known the example of cadet officers before them, and the body of the Corps had a most imperfect idea of the standards of bearing and conduct which have been characteristic of the cadet for over a century. The Old West Point could not be recognized as it appeared in June 1919. It had gone; it had to be replaced.

We had however many things in our favor: the buildings and equipment for a great military institution; the traditions of the Old West Point implanted in the character of its graduates; the experience of the World War to point the way; the assurance of loyal and devoted service from the fine corps of officers on duty here; and we soon had a point of departure in the legal establishment of a four-year course of study and training. Our problem was to build upon these foundations, and, with these guides and aids, a new West Point which would continue the fine tradition of the old and would give the most thorough preparation of officer personnel for possible future war: to deliver a product trained with a view to teaching, leading, and inspiring the modern citizen, in crises, to become an effective officer or soldier.

Our plan was fundamentally based upon what might be euphemistically called democracy-in-action. It has ever been a source of pride to those interested in West Point that the democracy of the Corps assured every individual cadet a standing won by his character and personality, irrespective of his social or financial position outside the walls of the institution. Every member of the student body throughout his four-year course wears the same clothes, eats the same food, passes through the same course of study, rises and retires at the same hours, receives the same pay, and starts always without handicap in the same competition.

The highest standards of honor were to be demanded as the only solid foundation for a military career—a code of individual conduct which would maintain the reputation and well-being of the whole—a personal responsibility to his mates, to his community, and above all to his country. In many businesses and professions the welfare of the individual is the chief object, but in the military profession the safety and honor of the state becomes paramount. In the final analysis of the West Point product, character is the most precious component.

Much criticism of narrowness and provincialism had been directed at the military academy in the past due to the restrictive range of interests possible for cadets during four important, formative years of their lives. They had no opportunity to familiarize themselves with the mores and standards of people in the world without, so that when they graduated and mingled freely with their fellows, they had no common background of knowledge and awareness. They were thrust out into the world, a man in age, but as experienced as a high school boy. They were cloistered almost to a monastic extent.

It was felt that this vacuum could be filled by allowing certain privileges common to all higher institutions of learning. This would serve both as a relaxation from the rigid grind of study and training, and as a means of keeping touch with life outside the walls of the institution. They no longer were to be walled up within the Academy limits, but were to be treated as responsible young men.

An important change in the military training system was the removal of the cadets from West Point to a regular army encampment for the summer period. Until this time, summer encampment had been limited to a week's artillery practice for first classmen. Under this new system, the cadets were brought into direct contact with actual service conditions during this important period of their military training. They gain in those qualities of self-confidence and assurance which are so valuable to efficient leadership. They learn more of human nature, acquire understanding, sympathy, and tact. The entire experience both broadens and deepens their character.

The problem of athletic training was one close to my heart. For many years, athletics at West Point had consisted of an excellent system of military gymnastics, but it was apparent from the experiences of the World War that a course of training should be planned not only to fit future officers physically for the rigors of military service, but also to qualify them as physical directors and instructors for their future commands. They must learn, not only how to perform themselves, but how to teach others. They must understand the means by which they can most speedily and efficiently bring their men to the necessary physical condition. They must appreciate the practical details of physical instruction and be qualified to stimulate and inspire, as well as perform.

In the old course, athletics was a voluntary activity. Only those cadets engaged in sports who were spurred by the ambition to gain a place on the team, or who played simply for pleasure. But the war had shown the value of organized group athletics in creating and maintaining morale. The effect upon the army at large of an extensive system of competitive sports, controlled by competent and well-prepared officers, cannot be overestimated. Troops in poor physical condition are worthless. It was evident that the problem of creating a model course in physical training and athletics at this great military school was vital. And it was equally evident that such a project could not fail to have a marked influence on the broad question of the physical qualifications of the youth of the nation.

Accordingly, it was decided that every cadet would be required to participate in all major sports under the supervision of qualified instructors. Mass athletics was to be taught and practiced in the sports of football, baseball, basketball, soccer, lacrosse, track, tennis, golf, and hockey as part of the regular curriculum. Cadets were first divided into small sections of twenty-five for preliminary training, and intramural contests between companies and battalions followed. Nothing brings out the qualities of leadership, mental and muscular co-ordination, aggressiveness, and courage more quickly than this type of competition. Physical qualities may well determine the destiny of the intellect. To emphasize these truths I had carved on the stone portals of the gymnasium these words:

> "Upon the fields of friendly strife
> Are sown the seeds
> That, upon other fields, on other days
> Will bear the fruits of victory"

Top:
Corps Commander Major General
Douglas MacArthur with Lieutenant Colonel
William B. Scres, Fort Howard, Maryland.
1927.

Bottom:
En route to Amsterdam
with the United States
Olympic Team.
1928.

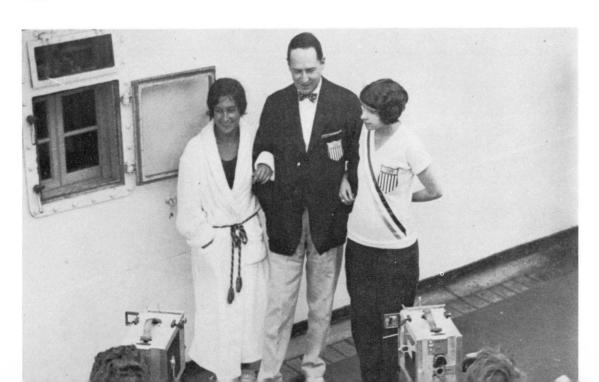

Day after day, for long hours, I huddled with the Academic Board in formulating and applying these plans of revitalization. We consulted with the leading university and military figures of the country. We sent our instructors to take courses in the greatest colleges throughout the land; adapted military courses to modern needs; scientific courses were brought up to date; classical courses were used as cultural foundations; a new course on economics and government was added; increased emphasis on history and world trends; studies into European conditions and the Far East; modern science, chemistry, electricity, aerodynamics, mechanics, languages, and a course of physical, mental, and moral training which we believed unexcelled by any institution in the world.

If the policies conceived and the means taken for their application were to be successful, if West Point was to incorporate the new without displacing the proven good of the old, it was necessary to submit our plans to the best critics the country could offer. The press, without exception, expressed enthusiastic approval of the changes. The Secretary of War was in accord. The majority of the senior officers of the Army approved. Ninety-one distinguished educators studied the plans, and from none came adverse criticism of the new foundations we were laying. The Board of Visitors, composed of seven members of the United States House of Representatives, reported: "The Board desires to emphasize its strong approval of the splendid service that General MacArthur and the officers associated with him are rendering to the country by constructing a new West Point, founded on the lessons and experiences and the sacrifices of the World War, and in the spirit of Old West Point."

In January 1920,

I was appointed a brigadier general in the Regular Army. Late in 1922, being at the top of the roster of general officers for foreign service, I was relieved as superintendent and ordered to the Philippine Islands.

It has been a source of deepest satisfaction to me to know how successful have been the cadets who were at the academy during my tour as superintendent. Of those handsome, slim boys in gray, two, Lyman Lemnitzer and Maxwell Taylor, became chairman of the Joint Chiefs of Staff; two others, Hoyt Vandenberg and Thomas White, be-

Above:
Brigadier General Douglas MacArthur in the Philippines. 1922.

Facing page:
Manila. 1930.

Above: Taking the oath of office
as Chief of Staff of the Army.
"Now the responsibility of making
decisions and giving the orders was mine."

Below left: With Major General Craig,
MacArthur's successor as Ninth
Corps Commander. 1930.
Below right: With King Carol of Rumania.

Above:
MacArthur's first official
review as Chief of Staff.
Below: France.

Above:
Bucharest.

Facing page, top:
Warsaw.

Facing page, bottom:
Yugoslavia.

Above: Yugoslavia.

Facing page:
France, with General Henri Gouraud.
"The greatest of them all."

Right top: France.

Right bottom: Receiving honorary
degree of Doctor of Laws.
Pittsburgh University. 1932.

came chiefs of staff of the Air Corps, and so many became general officers that it would be in vain to attempt to recount them. The worth of such men to the country is without price.

During the years 1922–31 MacArthur rose from brigadier general to Chief of Staff. In addition to his service in the Philippines attempting to organize inadequate numbers of men and material to combat the growing menace of the Japanese, MacArthur also served on the courts-martial board that heard the case of Billy Mitchell—America's first champion of air power. It was MacArthur's vote that saved Mitchell from dismissal.

Assuming the post of Chief of Staff, he continued to campaign for adequate military appropriations for the war he knew was coming. His unrelenting efforts for military preparedness gained him the enmity of those groups anxious to believe that war would come no more.

The most poignant episode during my role as Chief of Staff was the so-called Bonus March. The country was in the third year of the great Depression, and heartache and hunger haunted the millions of unemployed. Men lost faith, and the spirit of the country sank to a low that had not been experienced since the financial panic of 1892. Late in May, an army of disillusioned and lost men who had served in the war, the vanguard of a starved band, arrived in Washington, seeking desperately to influence the Congress to grant an immediate cash bonus for veterans. For two fruitless months they lived in abject squalor, making their daily marches to the Capitol, to the White House, and to all of the other sacrosanct federal buildings where they hoped to loosen the purse-strings of government. In the end, their frustration combined with careful needling by the Communists, turned them into a sullen, riotous mob.

In these days of wholehearted national unity, it is hard to believe that thirty years ago the President of the United States lived in danger, and that Congress shook with fear at the sight and sound of the marchers. It is hard to believe, too, that government employees and other citizens of Washington who bore witness to the tawdry street battles cheered the stoning of the Washington police force.

The movement was actually far deeper and more dangerous than an effort to secure funds from a nearly depleted federal treasury. The American Communist Party planned a riot of such proportions that it was hoped the United States Army, in its efforts to maintain peace, would have to fire on the marchers. In this way, the Communists hoped to incite revolutionary action. Red organizers infiltrated the veteran groups and presently took command from their unwitting leaders.

Walter W. Waters, a persuasive ex-serviceman from Oregon with a gift for public speaking, was the leader of the Bonus Marchers. I conferred with him and reached an agreement that if the Army was called in, he would withdraw the veterans without violence. Many of them were bedded down in partly demolished buildings along Pennsylvania Avenue. To provide further shelter, I issued tents and camp equipment to be set up on the Anacostia Flats. I also ordered out a number of rolling kitchens to relieve any acute suffering. This latter step raised an outburst in Congress. A leader in the House of Representatives said from the floor:

If they come to Washington, sit down and have three meals furnished free every day, then God knows what will happen to us. There are more than 8,500,000 persons out of work in the United States, most of them with families. If the Government can feed those that are here, then we can expect an influx that will startle the whole country.

The rolling kitchens were withdrawn.

Senator J. Hamilton Lewis inspected the tired and, in some cases, shoeless veterans lying around the Capitol Building and then told his colleagues in the Senate that, "By abandoning the plea for justice and adopting in its place threat and coercion, veterans are causing fellow countrymen to wonder whether their soldiers served for patriotism or merely for pay."

Through the month of June the tension mounted. The camps now occupied by an estimated 17,000 spread out to every sizeable vacant lot. At night, morose men squatted by burning campfires listening silently to the endless speeches, always tinged with the increasing violence of Communist propaganda. The privations, the punishing heat, the unsanitary living conditions, and the interminable hours of wishful waiting for the slightly more than one thousand dollars which was to be each man's share—if Congress relented —took its toll.

During June, the governor of New York, Frank-

The Bonus march.
"The most poignant episode
during my role
as Chief of Staff."

lin D. Roosevelt, informed New Yorkers among the Bonus Marchers that the state would pay their railroad fares if they left Washington immediately and returned to New York. President Hoover got a bill through Congress authorizing loans for transportation, and most of the real veterans left. But the hard core of the Communist bloc not only stayed, but grew. The Federal Bureau of Investigation reported that an examination of the fingerprints of 4,723 Bonus Marchers showed that 1,069 of them were men who had criminal records ranging from drunkenness to murder and rape. Not more than one in ten of those who stayed was a veteran. By this time Waters had been deposed and the Communists had gained control.

As the violence increased, Pelham Glassford, commander of the Washington police, twice consulted with me about calling on the Army for assistance. Both times I advised against it. But on July 28th, the crisis was reached. A mob 5,000 strong began to move up Pennsylvania Avenue toward the Treasury Building and the White House. The police were outnumbered five to one. Glassford was mauled and stripped of his police superintendent's gold badge, gunfire broke out, two men were killed and a score or more badly injured. It was evident that the situation had gotten beyond the control of the local authorities.

A request was immediately made through the Board of Commissioners of the District of Columbia for federal troops. Commissioner Richelderfer, in requesting such assistance from the President, stated that it would "be impossible for the police department to maintain law and order except by the free use of firearms. The presence of federal troops in small number will obviate the seriousness of the situation, and it will result in far less violence and bloodshed."

The President then conferred with Patrick Hurley, the Secretary of War, who was immediately placed in charge. Hurley issued the following order:

To: General Douglas MacArthur
    Chief of Staff, U.S. Army.
    The President has just now informed me that the civil government of the District of Columbia has reported to him that it is unable to maintain law and order in the District.
    You will have United States troops proceed immediately to the scene of disorder. Cooperate fully with the District of Columbia police force which is now in charge. Surround the affected area and clear it without delay.

Turn over all prisoners to the civil authorities.

In your orders insist that any women or children who may be in the affected area be accorded every consideration and kindness. Use all humanity consistent with the due execution of the order.

Patrick J. Hurley,
Secretary of War.

Six hundred soldiers under the command of General Perry L. Miles had been drawn from units close to Washington. General Miles' orders to his unit commanders were as follows:

We are acting on the order of the President of the United States. The cavalry will make a demonstration down Pennsylvania Avenue. The infantry will deploy in line of skirmishers in the rear of the cavalry. You will surround the area and evict the men in possession there. Use care and consideration toward all women and children who may be in the area.

In accordance with the President's request, I accompanied General Miles and brought with me two officers who later wrote their names on world history: Major Dwight D. Eisenhower and Major George S. Patton.

Not a shot was fired. The sticks, clubs, and stones of the rioters were met only by tear gas and steady pressure. No one was killed and there were no serious injuries on either side. By 9:30 P.M. the area was cleared as far as the Anacostia Flats. The show of force, the excellent discipline of the troops, and the proper use of tear gas had turned the trick without serious bloodshed. At Anacostia Flats I received word from the Secretary of War, as we were in the midst of crossing the river, to suspend the operation at my discretion. I halted the command as soon as we had cleared the bridge, but at that moment the rioters set fire to their own camp. This concluded the proceedings for the night.

I personally reported to the President and Secretary Hurley at the White House about eleven o'clock, and they expressed gratification at what had been accomplished. Secretary Hurley asked me to give a statement to the waiting newspaper men. After explaining the events of the preceding day, I continued:

If President Hoover had not acted when he did he would have been faced with a serious situation. Another week might have meant that the government was in peril. He had reached the end of an extraordinary patience and had gone to the very limit to avoid friction before using force. Had the President not acted when he did he would have been derelict in his duty.

Testifying on
the unemployment
relief plan before
the House Labor Committee.

The day following the riot, the police rounded up thirty-six of the leaders, including James Ford, the American Communist Party candidate for Vice-President; Emmanual Levin, a leading New York Communist; and John T. Pace, an acknowledged former Communist. This broke up the organization, and its remnants disappeared.

The most extravagant distortions of what had occurred were widely circulated. I was violently attacked, and even blatantly misrepresented before Congress. Speeches pictured me in full dress uniform astride a fiery white charger, bedecked with medals, waving a bloody saber, and leading a mad cavalry charge against unarmed and innocent citizens. Of course there was absolutely no foundation for such statements. There was no cavalry charge. There was no fiery white charger. There was no saber. There was no full dress uniform. There were no medals. I wore the same uniform as the troops. When I challenged such distortions, they were merely shrugged off with the expression, "it was only politics." Franklin Roosevelt once said to me, "Douglas, I think you are our best general, but I believe you would be our worst politician." With his rare sense of humor, I wonder which side of that remark he thought was the compliment.

Three days after the uprising, *The New York Times,* in a front-page account, reported:

The Communist Party, at its Headquarters here, accepted responsibility yesterday for the demonstration that resulted in the bonus-army riots in Washington.

"We agitated for the bonus and led the demonstration of the veterans in Washington," a spokesman for the party said at the headquarters at 50 East 13th Street. "We stand ready to go to Washington again and fight for the working men. We started the march from here for Washington and we will lead the way again!"

In 1948, more of the Communist conspiracy was revealed when Benjamin Gitlow, an admitted Communist, wrote in his book, *The Whole of Their Lives:*

On July 5 Earl Browder declared that the veterans were the shock troops of the unemployed. Said he, "The Bonus revolutionary force in Washington is the most significant beginning of the mass struggle against the deepening consequences of the crisis."

On July 28 the government went into action. General Douglas MacArthur, Chief of Staff of the United States Army, stepped in to prevent serious bloodshed after a fight between communist led vet-

Above:
With Secretary of War
George Dern, Camp Dix.
"At a time when Hitler was still
popularly regarded as a windbag,
Japan publicized as a fake,
and our government promising it
would forever keep us out of war,
we formed the central character
of the United States Army
of World War II."

Facing page, top:
Conference with general officers,
Camp Dix.

Facing page, bottom:
With Dwight D. Eisenhower.

Below:
The Philippines, June, 1934
through 1937. Commanding General,
Philippine Depot.

Above:
With Manuel Quezon,
first President of
the Philippine Commonwealth.

Facing page, top:
Accepting a commission
as field marshal
in the Philippine Army.

Facing page, bottom:
With the Philippine
Boy Scouts.

Facing page:
At the time of
MacArthur's marriage
to Jean Marie Faircloth.
"It was perhaps
the smartest thing
I've ever done."

Through the years.

Above:
Receiving honorary degree
from the University of
the Philippines. 1938.

Below:
Manila, shortly after
the birth of Arthur
MacArthur.

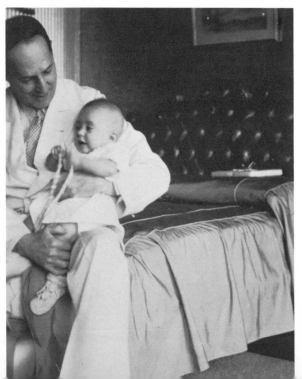

erans and police resulting in the death of one veteran and the shooting of an innocent bystander. It was just what the communists wanted. It is what they had conspired to bring about. Now they could brand Hoover as a murderer of hungry unemployed veterans. They could charge that the United States Army was Wall Street's tool with which to crush the unemployed and that the government and the Congress of the United States were bloody Fascist butchers of unarmed American workmen.

In 1949, John T. Pace testified under oath before a Congressional committee:

> I feel responsible in part for the oft repeated lie about President Hoover and General MacArthur.
>
> I led the left wing or communist section of the bonus march. I was ordered by my Red superiors to provoke riots. I was told to use every trick to bring about bloodshed in the hopes that President Hoover would be forced to call out the army. The communists didn't care how many veterans were killed. I was told Moscow had ordered riots and bloodshed in the hopes that this might set off the revolution. My communist bosses were jumping with joy on July 28 when the Washington police killed one veteran. The Army was called out by President Hoover and didn't fire a shot or kill a man. General MacArthur put down a Moscow directed revolution without bloodshed, and that's why the communists hate him.

During the Bonus March Communist threats continued to be made against responsible officials. I was to be publicly hanged on the steps of the Capitol. It was the beginning of a definite and ceaseless campaign that set me apart as a man to be destroyed, no matter how long the Communists and their friends and admirers had to wait, and no matter what means they might have to use. But it was to be nineteen years before the bells of Moscow pealed out their glee at my eclipse.

During the fall of 1941

the signs of impending conflict with the Japanese became unmistakably clear. I prepared my meager forces, to counter as best I might, the attack that I knew would come from the north, swiftly, fiercely, and without warning.

The Japanese strategic objectives (later determined by captured war records) were complete hegemony in Asia and unchallenged supremacy in the western Pacific. This involved the immediate conquest and subjugation of the Philippines and the capture of the immense natural resources of the Netherlands East Indies and Malaya. The islands represented America's single hope of effective resistance in Southeast Asia, and, given the time and resources, the Philippine Defense Plan would accomplish its long-range objective of making them too costly in men and dollars to attack. Lieutenant General Torashiro Kawabe, deputy chief of the Japanese general staff, joined by Lieutenant General Akira Muto, director of the military affairs bureau of the war ministry, and Lieutenant Colonel Hikaru Haba, intelligence staff, Fourteenth Army, stated that

> . . . an important factor in Japan's decision to invade the Philippines was the fear on the part of the Japanese General Staff of the ten-year plan for the defense of the Philippines. The plan was in its sixth year and a potential menace to Japan's ambitions. The Japanese had to intervene before it was too late.

During one of my staff conferences I had once called the Philippines "the Key that unlocks the door to the Pacific." The Japanese understood this completely, for the Philippines, although not economically necessary to Japan's grandiose scheme, were close to South China and the island stronghold of Formosa, forming not only an obstacle to Japan's international ambitions, but depriving the Rising Sun of a powerful strategic springboard for their drive south and eastward. Flanking the vital sea routes to the south, they were the hub of the transportation system to Southeast Asia and the Southwest Pacific and a direct line of communication to Java, Malaya, Borneo, and New Guinea.

The Japanese planned to isolate the region by destroying Allied naval power in the Pacific and Far Eastern waters, thus severing British and American lines of communication with the Orient. The unsupported garrisons of the Far East would then be overwhelmed and the areas marked for conquest quickly seized. Air attacks launched from progressively advanced airfields would prepare the way for amphibious assaults.

The first major operation would be a crippling attack against the American fleet at Pearl Harbor, followed immediately by advances directed against the Philippines and Malaya, with the invasion of British Borneo following as soon as possible. In the early stages of these campaigns, other striking forces were to seize objectives in Celebes, Dutch Borneo, and southern Sumatra, enabling the forward concentration of aircraft to support the invasion of Java. After the fall of Singapore,

northern Sumatra would be occupied, and operations would also be carried out against Burma at an appropriate time in order to cut the Allied supply routes to China. Singapore, Soerabaja, and Manila were expected to become major bases.

The Japanese plan involved the capture of other strategic areas where advance posts could be established, and an outer barrier raised against an Allied counter-offensive. Their scheme of conquest envisaged control of the Aleutians, Midway, Fiji and Samoa, New Britain, New Guinea, points in the Australian area, and the Andaman Islands in the Bay of Bengal. All these would be seized or neutralized when operational conditions permitted.

If the offensive succeeded, the United States would be forced back to Hawaii, the British to India, and China's lifeline would be cut. With this eminently favorable strategic situation and control of the raw materials which they required, the Japanese felt they would be in a position to prosecute the war to a successful conclusion and realize their ambition to dominate the Far East.

My forces were grouped into a number of major commands. The North Luzon Force, under the command of General Jonathan Wainwright, was the most important, being responsible for the defense of the landing beaches at Aparri and Vigan, and the exposed shores of Lingayen Gulf, some 110 miles north of Manila. The South Luzon Force, under General Jones, covered the coast from Batangas to Legaspi. The Lucena Force, under General Parker, defended the Bicol Peninsula. The Visayan Force, under General Chenoywith, had the central island group, and the Mindanao Force, under General William F. Sharpe, was responsible for that entire island. Corregidor and the harbor defenses were commanded by General Moore, and the Air Force by Major General Lewis H. Brereton. The chief of artillery was General King.

My staff was unsurpassed in excellence, and comprised such outstanding figures as Sutherland, the chief of staff; Marshall in Supply; Casey of the Engineers; Willoughby in Intelligence; Aiken in Communications; Marquat in Artillery. No commander was ever better served.

On November 21st, upon the recommendation of General Brereton, our Bombardment Group of B-17s was moved from Clark Field to Delmonte Field in Mindanao, in order to place it beyond the range of attack from Formosa. Actually, only half of them were withdrawn. I never learned why these orders were not promptly implemented. I realized only too well how small the protecting force of fighters was and how helpless practically undefended Clark Field, with no dispersal areas, would be against heavy air attack.

My orders from Washington were not to initiate hostilities against the Japanese under any circumstances. The first overt move in the Philippine area must come from the enemy. There was apparently some hope that the somewhat indeterminate international position of the commonwealth might eliminate it from attack. This possibility had support not only from President Manuel Quezon, but from the American chief of staff.

Our pursuit interceptor planes began night patrols on December 4th in territorial waters which extended well out to sea. Each night they located Japanese bombers from 20 to 50 miles out, but these presumed enemy planes turned back before the international line was reached. The last of these night flights was intercepted and turned back at the exact time of the attack on Pearl Harbor.

Whatever might come, we were as ready as we possibly could be in our inadequate defenses, on the night of December 7th. Every disposition had been made, every man, gun, and plane was on the alert.

Facing page:
Pearl Harbor.
Wreckage of the USS *Arizona*.
December 7, 1941.

Part III

World War II

December 8, 1941,

at 3:40 A.M. Manila time, a long-distance telephone call from Washington told me of the Japanese attack on Pearl Harbor, but no details were
given. It was our strongest military position in the
Pacific. Its garrison was a mighty one, with America's best aircraft on strongly defended fields, adequate warning systems, anti-aircraft batteries,
backed up by our Pacific Fleet. My first impression
was that the Japanese might well have suffered a
serious setback.

We had only one radar station operative and
had to rely for air warning largely on eye and ear.
At 9:30 A.M. our reconnaissance planes reported
a force of enemy bombers over Lingayen Gulf
heading toward Manila. Major General Lewis H.
Brereton, who had complete tactical control of
the Far East Air Force, immediately ordered pursuit planes up to intercept them. But the enemy
bombers veered off without contact.

When this report reached me, I was still
under the impression that the Japanese had suffered a setback at Pearl Harbor, and their failure
to close in on me supported that belief. I therefore contemplated an air reconnaissance to the
north, using bombers with fighter protection, to
ascertain a true estimate of the situation and
to exploit any possible weaknesses that might
develop on the enemy's front. But subsequent
events quickly and decisively changed my mind.
I learned, to my astonishment, that the Japanese
had succeeded in their Hawaiian attack, and at
11:45 a report came in of an overpowering enemy
formation closing in on Clark Field. Our fighters
went up to meet them, but our bombers were slow
in taking off and our losses were heavy. Our
force was simply too small to smash the odds
against them.

*With the Navy unable to maintain MacArthur's
supply lines the Japanese commenced large-scale*

landings of troops and materials. Attempting a series of pincer movements, the Japanese envisaged complete annihilation of the Luzon defense force within a short period of time. Pitting his own knowledge of the terrain against the Japanese superiority in air power, tanks, artillery, and men, MacArthur fought a series of delaying movements toward Corregidor.

On Christmas Eve, Manila was evacuated and headquarters were moved to Corregidor.

Our headquarters, called "Topside," occupied the flattened summit of the highest hill on the island. It gave a perfect view of the whole panorama of the siege area. As always, I had to see the enemy or I could not fight him effectively. Reports, no matter how penetrating, have never been able to replace the picture shown to my eyes. The Filipinos, even as the smoke pillars of their burning villages dotted the land, were being told that Europe came first. Angry frustration, for citizens and soldiers alike, irritated bruised nerves and increased the sense of heartache and loss. And the enemy, night after night, in the seductive voice of "Tokyo Rose," rubbed the raw wounds by telling them over the radio that defeat and death were to be their fate while America's aid went elsewhere. President Quezon was stunned by the reports of the huge amounts of American supplies now being sent to Russia. His expression of bewildered anger was something I can never forget. As an evidence of assurance to these people suffering from deprivation, destruction, and despair, I deemed it advisable to locate headquarters as prominently as possible, notwithstanding exposure to enemy attack.

They came in a perfect formation of twin-engine bombers, glittering in the brilliant blue sky. Far-off, they looked like silver pieces thrown against the sun. But their currency was death and their appearance a deceit. These were deadly weapons of war and their bomb bays contained a terrible force of destruction. The long white main barracks, a concrete straight line, cracked and splintered like a glass box. The tin edges of the overhanging roof, under the impact of a thousand pounder, were bent upward like the curvature of a Chinese pagoda. Pieces of the metal whirled through the air like bits of macabre confetti. A 500-pound burst took off the roof of my quarters. Telephone lines snapped and coiled to the ground. The sturdy rails and ties of the local streetcar line were loosed and looped up into meaningless form. The lawn became a gaping, smoking crater. Blue sky turned to dirty gray.

Then came strafing, and again the bombing. Always they followed the same pattern. Their own orders could not have enlightened me more. What I learned, I used to advantage later. They kept it up for three hours. The din was ferocious. The peaceful chirping of birds had been replaced by the shrill scream of dive bombers. The staccato of strafing was answered by the pounding of the anti-aircraft batteries. Machine guns chattered everywhere and ceaselessly. Then they left as shaking earth yielded under this pulverizing attack, and there rose a slow choking cover of dust and smoke and flame.

My new headquarters was located in an arm of the Malinta Tunnel. Carved deep in the rock, the central tunnel was actually the terminal point of a streetcar line. Other passages had been hewn out of the rock and these now housed hospital wards, storerooms, and ammunition magazines. The headquarters was bare, glaringly lighted, and contained only the essential furniture and equipment for administrative procedure. At the sound of the air alarm, an aide and I would make our way out through the crowded civilians seeking shelter in the main passageway, huddled silently in that hunched-down, age-old Oriental squat of patience and stolid resignation, onto the highway to watch the weaving pattern of the enemy's formations.

There was nothing of bravado in this. It was simply my duty. The gunners at the batteries, the men in the foxholes, they too were in the open. They liked to see me with them at such moments. The subtle corrosion of panic or fatigue, or the feeling of just being fed up, can only be arrested by the intervention of the leader. Leadership is often crystallized in some sort of public gesture. For example, in peace, such a gesture might be the breaking of bread as a symbol of hospitality, or with native Indians, the smoking of a peace pipe to show friendship. But in war, to be effective it must take the form of a fraternity of danger welded between a commander and his troops by the common denominator of sharing the risk of sudden death.

Our troops were now approaching exhaustion. The guerrilla movement was going well, but on Bataan and Corregidor the clouds were growing darker. My heart ached as I saw my men slowly wasting away. Their clothes hung on them like tattered rags. Their bare feet stuck out in silent protest. Their long bedraggled hair framed gaunt bloodless faces. Their hoarse, wild laughter greeted the constant stream of obscene and ribald jokes issuing from their parched, dry throats. They cursed the enemy and in the same breath cursed and reviled the United States; they spat when they jeered at the Navy. But their eyes would light up and they would cheer when they saw my battered, and much reviled in America, "scrambled egg" cap. They would gather round and pat me on the back and "Mabuhay Macarsar" me. They would grin—that ghastly skeleton-like grin of the dying—as they would roar in unison, "We are the battling bastards of Bataan—no papa, no mama, no Uncle Sam."

They asked no quarter and they gave none. They died hard—those savage men—not gently like a stricken dove folding its wings in peaceful passing, but like a wounded wolf at bay, with lips curled back in sneering menace, and always a nerveless hand reaching for that long sharp machete knife which long ago they had substituted for the bayonet. And around their necks, as we buried them, would be a thread of dirty string with its dangling crucifix. They were filthy, and they were lousy, and they stank. And I loved them.

General Marshall had suggested that Mrs. MacArthur and Arthur be evacuated by submarine. The tactical picture was worsening almost minute by minute; this might be the last opportunity for sure deliverance of the two human beings dearest to me. The Quezons implored me to agree; they and the Sayres planned to leave at once. It was one of the desperate moments of my life, but even before I spoke to Jean I knew the answer. When I returned to the Quezons, I said simply, "She will stay with me to the end. We drink from the same cup." I heard the convulsive gasp of Doña Aurora, and Quezon's eyes filled, but they said no word. They understood.

I answered Marshall's sympathetic suggestion: "I and my family will share the fate of the garrison." The following day he responded that he was concerned by those words. His message contained the implication that a further assignment for me could very well force me from my family, under conditions of even greater danger, and from the valiant garrison whose fate I had pledged us to share.

The High Commissioner and Mrs. Sayre left on February 20th by submarine for Australia, followed by the Quezons. Manuel slipped the signet

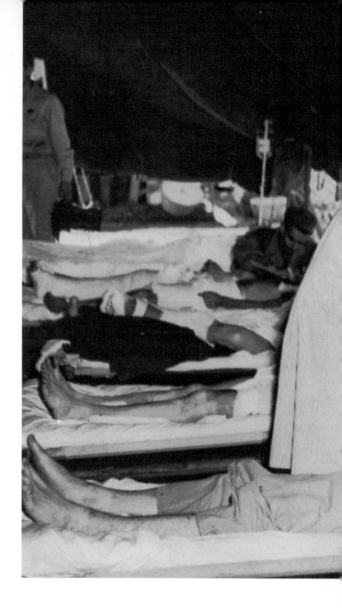

ring he always wore from his finger to mine, and said in broken words, "When they find your body, I want them to know you fought for my country." They were my son's godparents, and I held them in deepest affection.

On February 21st—Arthur's fourth birthday—Marshall notified me that the President was considering ordering me to Mindanao to set up a new base of operations for the defense of the southern part of the Philippines. The same day the cabinet in Canberra had requested my immediate assignment to Australia as commander of the newly formed Southwest Pacific Area. When Prime Minister Curtin's recommendation reached the White House, President Roosevelt personally sent me a message to proceed as soon as possible to Mindanao. There I was to do what I could to buttress defenses, then go on to Australia.

My first reaction was to try and avoid the latter part of the order, even to the extent of resigning my commission and joining the Bataan force as a simple volunteer. But Dick Sutherland and my entire staff would have none of it.

I decided to try and pierce the blockade with PT boats rather than go under with a submarine. The PT's, 77 feet of light plywood, under the command of Lieutenant John D. Bulkeley, were powered by Packard motors which had been slowed below top performance of 40 knots by long and arduous service, but were still capable of giving a Japanese cruiser or destroyer a run for its money. Bulkeley ordered the boats into roughly a diamond formation that would afford the best position for launching any of the sixteen torpedoes, each capable of sinking a destroyer or a cruiser. The plan was to attack at once if we were sighted by Japanese surface craft, sending out a co-ordinated salvo of torpedo fire. After that we would have to depend on our superior, high-speed maneuverability.

I sent for General Wainwright, who was to be left in command to tell him goodbye. He had been a plebe at West Point when I was a first classman and later became the First Captain of the Class of 1906. A fine soldierly figure, he had already done wonders in the campaign, and was popular with both officers and men. "Jim," I told him, "hold on till I come back for you." I was to come back, but it would be too late—too late for those battling men in the foxholes of Bataan, too late for the valiant gunners at the batteries of Corregidor, too late for Jim Wainwright.

It was 7:15 on the evening of March 11th

Mrs. MacArthur visits
the wounded. Manila.

when I walked across the porch to my wife. "Jean," I said gently, "it is time to go." We drove in silence to the South Dock, where Bulkeley and PT-41 were waiting; the rest of the party was already aboard. Shelling of the waterfront had continued intermittently all day. I put Jean, Arthur and Ah Cheu on board, and then turned slowly to look back.

On the dock I could see the men staring at me. I had lost 25 pounds living on the same diet as the soldiers, and I must have looked gaunt and ghastly standing there in my old war-stained clothes—no bemedaled commander of inspiring presence. What a change had taken place in that once-beautiful spot! My eyes roamed that warped and twisted face of scorched rock. Gone was the vivid green foliage, with its trees, shrubs, and flowers. Gone were the buildings, the sheds, every growing thing. The hail of relentless bombardment had devastated, buried, and blasted. Ugly dark scars marked smouldering paths where the fire had raged from one end of the island to the other. Great gaps and forbidding crevices still belched their tongues of flame. The desperate scene showed only a black mass of destruction. Through the shattered ruins, my eyes sought "Topside," where the deep roar of the heavy guns still growled defiance, with their red blasts tearing the growing darkness asunder. Up there, in command, was my classmate, Paul Bunker. Forty years had passed since Bunker had been twice selected by Walter Camp for the All-American team. I could shut my eyes and see again that blond head racing, tearing, plunging—210 pounds of irresistible power. I could almost hear Quarterback Charley Daly's shrill voice barking, "Bunker back." He and many others up there were old, old friends, bound by ties of deepest comradeship.

Darkness had now fallen, and the waters were beginning to ripple from the faint night breeze. The enemy firing had ceased and a muttering silence had fallen. It was as though the dead were passing by the stench of destruction. The smell of filth thickened the night air. I raised my cap in farewell salute, and I could feel my face go white, feel a sudden, convulsive twitch in the muscles of my face. I heard someone ask, "What's his chance, Sarge, of getting through?" and the gruff reply, "Dunno. He's lucky. Maybe one in five."

I stepped aboard PT-41. "You may cast off, Buck," I said, "when you are ready."

Although the flotilla consisted of only four battle-scarred PT boats, its size was no gauge of

Above:
Awarding the Distinguished
Service Cross to Capt. Jesus Villamor
of the Philippine Air Force.
"Our air force was hopelessly
outnumbered and never had
a chance of winning."

Facing page: 1941.

the uniqueness of its mission. This was the desperate attempt by a commander-in-chief and his key staff to move thousands of miles through the enemy's lines to another war theater, to direct a new and intensified assault. Nor did the Japanese themselves underestimate the significance of such a movement. "Tokyo Rose" had announced gleefully that, if captured, I would be publicly hanged on the Imperial Plaza in Tokyo, where the Imperial towers overlooked the traditional parade ground of the Emperor's Guard divisions. Little did I dream that bleak night that five years later, at the first parade review of Occupation troops, I would take the salute as supreme commander for the Allied Powers on the precise spot so dramatically predicted for my execution.

The tiny convoy rendezvoused at Turning Buoy just outside the minefield at 8 P.M. Then we roared through in single file, Bulkeley leading and Admiral Rockwell in PT-34 closing the formation.

On the run to Cabra Island, many white lights were sighted—the enemy's signal that a break was being attempted through the blockade. The noise of our engines had been heard, but the sound of a PT engine is hard to differentiate from that of a bomber, and they evidently mistook it. Several boats passed. The sea rose and it began to get rough. Spiteful waves slapped and snapped at the thin skin of the little boats; visibility was becoming poorer.

As we began closing on the Japanese blockading fleet, the suspense grew tense. Suddenly, there they were, sinister outlines against the curiously peaceful formations of lazily drifting cloud. We waited, hardly breathing, for the first burst of shell that would summon us to identify ourselves. Ten seconds. Twenty. A full minute. No gun spoke; the PT's rode so low in the choppy seas that they had not spotted us.

Bulkeley changed at once to a course that brought us to the west and north of the enemy craft, and we slid by in the darkness. Again and again, this was to be repeated during the night, but our luck held.

The weather deteriorated steadily, and towering waves buffeted our tiny, war-weary, blacked-out vessels. The flying spray drove against our skin like stinging pellets of birdshot. We would fall off into a trough, then climb up the near slope of a steep water peak, only to slide down the other side. The boat would toss crazily back and forth, seeming to hang free in space as though about to breach, and then would break away and

Above:
1942.

Below:
Corregidor.
With Francis Sayre,
United States
High Commissioner
to the Philippines.

go forward with a rush. I recall describing the experience afterward as what it must be like to take a trip in a concrete mixer. The four PT's could no longer keep formation, and by 3:30 A.M. the convoy had scattered. Bulkeley tried for several hours to collect the others, but without success. Now each skipper was on his own, his rendezvous just off the uninhabited Cuyo Islands.

It was a bad night for everybody. At dawn, Lieutenant (j.g.) V. E. Schumacher, commander of PT-32, saw what he took for a Jap destroyer bearing down at 30 knots through the early morning fog. The torpedo tubes were instantly cleared for action, and the 600-gallon gasoline drums jettisoned to lighten the vessel when the time came to make a run for it. Just before the signal to fire, the onrushing "enemy" was seen to be the PT-41—mine.

The first boat to arrive at Tagauayan at 9:30 on the morning of March 12 was PT-34, under the command of Lieutenant R. G. Kelly. PT-32 and Bulkeley's PT-41 arrived at approximately 4 P.M. with PT-32 running out of fuel; those aboard were placed on the two other already crowded craft. A submarine which had been ordered to join us at the Cuyos did not appear. We waited as the day's stifling heat intensified, still spots on the water camouflaged as well as possible from the prying eyes of searching enemy airmen. Hours passed and at last we could wait no longer for Ensign A. B. Akers' PT-35 (it arrived two hours after we left). I gave the order to move out southward into the Mindanao Sea for Cagayan, on the northern coast. This time Rockwell's boat led and PT-41 followed. The night was clear, the sea rough and high.

Once more, huge and hostile, a Japanese warship loomed dead ahead through the dark. We were too near to run, too late to dodge. Instantly we cut engines, cleared for action—and waited. Seconds ticked into minutes, but no signal flashed from the battleship as she steamed slowly westward across our path. If we had been seen at all, we had been mistaken for part of the native fishing fleet. Our road to safety was open.

We made it into Cagayan at 7 A.M. on Friday, March 13. I called together the officers and men of both PT's. "It was done in true naval style," I told them. "It gives me great pleasure and honor to award the boats' crews the Silver Star for gallantry for fortitude in the face of heavy odds."

Brigadier General William F. Sharp, commander of the Visayan Mindanao Force, greeted

Arthur MacArthur,
the General's son,
in Malinta Tunnel,
Corregidor.

me on landing, and reported all was well with his troop. Davao was in enemy hands, but if Bataan fell, his plans for intensified guerrilla warfare were well advanced.

Four B-17's from Australia had been scheduled to meet our party. One had crashed in the waters offshore, two never reached Cagayan, and the fourth was so dangerously decrepit that General Sharp had ordered it back empty to Australia before our arrival. Of three more planes dispatched for us, two arrived around 8 P.M. on March 16. They were in bad shape, tied together, as their pilots said, "with chewing gum and bailing wire." We took off from the Del Monte strip shortly after midnight on March 17th, the plane in which I was traveling rattling down the runway with one engine sparking and missing. We would be flying over enemy-held territory, relying on darkness to help us evade Japanese patrols. Over Timor, we were spotted and they came up after us. But we changed course from Darwin, where they figured we would land, and came in at Batchelor Field, 40 miles to the south, just as they hit the Darwin field. They discovered their mistake too late, and their dive bombers and fighters roared in at Batchelor ten minutes after I had left in another plane for Alice Spring to the south.

"It was close," I remarked to Dick Sutherland when we landed, "but that's the way it is in war. You win or lose, live or die—and the difference is just an eyelash."

When we arrived at Batchelor Field, reporters pressed me for a statement. I said: "The President of the United States ordered me to break through the Japanese lines and proceed from Corregidor to Australia for the purpose, as I understand it, of organizing the American offensive against Japan, a primary object of which is the relief of the Philippines. I came through and I shall return."

I spoke casually enough, but the phrase "I shall return" seemed a promise of magic to the Filipinos. It lit a flame that became a symbol which focused the nation's indomitable will and at whose shrine it finally attained victory and, once again, found freedom. It was scraped in the sands of the beaches, it was daubed on the walls of the *barrios*, it was stamped on the mail, it was whispered in the cloisters of the church. It became the battle cry of a great underground swell that no Japanese bayonet could still.

Continually rallying his forces with the prom-

Facing page:
Preparing to leave
Corregidor by PT boat.
"She will stay with me
to the end. We drink
from the same cup."

Arrival in Australia.
"I shall keep a soldier's faith."

Above left:
Honoring Australia's
war dead.

Facing page, top left:
Melbourne.

Facing page, top right:
With Brigadier General
Patrick Hurley.

Facing page, middle:
U.S. troops docking
in Australia.

Facing page, bottom:
With Prime Minister
John Curtin.

Below left:
With Lieutenant General
G. H. Brett and
Colonel Merle Smith.

Above: Mrs. MacArthur with
Mrs. Roosevelt and Sir Leslie Wilson,
Governor-General of
Queensland.

Below left: Mrs. MacArthur
and Arthur, Queensland, Australia.
Below right:
Receiving the Legion of Merit.

ise of eventual victory, MacArthur, aided by a decisive Allied naval victory off Midway Island, defeated the Japanese invader in the steaming jungles of New Guinea. Utilizing the now famous concepts of tri-phibious warfare and "leap-frogging," he began the long march back to the Philippines.

Late in July, 1944,

I received a summons from General Marshall to repair to Pearl Harbor for a conference. No intimation was given as to the identity of the personage with whom I was to confer or the subject to be discussed. I felt reasonably certain it was President Roosevelt, but as I had never before been invited to sit in on any of the big conferences, and in fact I never was again, I felt that something closely affecting me must be involved. I took no staff officers with me except personal aides-de-camp, and carried no plans or maps.

The President received me warmly and spoke generously of my campaigns. He was accompanied by his chief of staff, Admiral William D. Leahy, and a retinue of personages both military and civil. Admiral King had been there the day preceding, but had left before my arrival.

In the conference hall the Navy had a tremendous paraphernalia of maps, plans, manuscripts, statistics of all sorts, and other visual adjuncts. I began to realize I was to go it alone. Admiral Nimitz, with his fine sense of fair play, asked if I had been informed of the subject to be discussed, and if I had been asked to bring my important staff members. When I told him I had not, he seemed amazed and somewhat shocked.

President Roosevelt stated the general purpose of the conference, which was to determine the next phase of action against Japan. The Navy then presented its plan, which was to by-pass the Philippines and enter the Western Pacific to attack Formosa. For this purpose, all of my American forces, except a token group of two divisions and a few air squadrons, were to be transferred to the command of Admiral Nimitz, who was to continue to drive across the Central Pacific. By the summer of 1945, he would be ready to invade Formosa. Just how to neutralize and contain the 300,000 Japanese troops left in his rear in the Philippines was never clearly explained to me.

Admiral Nimitz put forth the Navy plan, but I was sure it was King's and not his own. By this time I knew why I had been included in the con-

Above:
Admiral Lord Louis Mountbatten conferring with Lieutenant General Joseph W. Stilwell somewhere on the Burma front.

Below:
MacArthur and his son. Australia.

Right and below right:
Inspecting Army camps
in Australia. "Australia's
actual military position had become
almost desperate. Its forces were
weak to an extreme, and
Japanese invasion was
momentarily expected."

Below left:
The way back.
"I decided that the moment
had come for a counter-drive
that would clean the enemy
from Eastern Papua."
With Major General
William H. Rupertus.

ference. The President apparently knew the general concept of the plan, but was evidently doubtful of it. He was entirely neutral in handling the discussion.

I was in total disagreement with the proposed plan, not only on strategic but psychological grounds. Militarily, I felt that if I could secure the Philippines, it would enable us to clamp an air and naval blockade on the flow of all supplies from the south to Japan, and thus, by paralyzing her industries, force her to early capitulation. I argued against the naval concept of frontal assault against the strongly held island positions of Iwo Jima or Okinawa. In my argument, I stressed that our losses would be far too heavy to justify the benefits to be gained by seizing these outposts. They were not essential to the enemy's defeat, and by cutting them off from supplies, they could be easily reduced and their effectiveness completely neutralized with negligible loss to ourselves. They were not in themselves possessed of sufficient resources to act as main bases in our advance.

In addition, I felt that Formosa, with a hostile population, might prove doubtful to serve as a base of attack against Japan itself. I was also critical of what I regarded as a major blunder in originally abandoning all effort to relieve the Philippines. I stated that had we had the will to do so, we could have opened the way to reinforce the Bataan and Corregidor garrisons, and probably not only saved the Philippines, but thereby stopped the enemy's advance eastward toward New Guinea and Australia. I felt that to sacrifice the Philippines a second time could not be condoned or forgiven.

I argued that it was not only a moral obligation to release this friendly possession from the enemy, now that it had become possible, but that to fail to do so would not be understandable to the Oriental mind. Not to do so, moreover, would result in death to the thousands of prisoners, including American women, children, and men civilians, held in Philippine concentration camps. Practically all of the 17,000,000 Filipinos remained loyal to the United States, and were undergoing the greatest privations and sufferings because we had not been able to support or succor them. To by-pass isolated islands was one thing, but to leave in your rear such a large enemy concentration as the Philippines involved serious and unnecessary risks. I invited attention to the fact that nothing had been said of the atitude of the War Department—that I could not understand why General Marshall's views were not presented.

The meeting adjourned until the following morning, with the President making no final decision. At this second meeting, I once again pointed out how necessary for the winning of the war was the recapture of Luzon, and how simple it would be, once Manila Bay and the northern part of Luzon were back in our hands, to deny Japan the oil, rubber, and rice she was presently draining out of the conquered areas along the shores of the South China Sea and farther south. The President interrupted: "But Douglas, to take Luzon would demand heavier losses than we can stand." "Mr. President," I replied, "my losses would not be heavy, anymore than they have been in the past. The days of the frontal attack should be over. Modern infantry weapons are too deadly, and frontal assault is only for mediocre commanders. Good commanders do not turn in heavy losses."

Then I sketched my own over-all plan for future operations in the Southwest Pacific. Once I held the Philippines, I would begin the reconquest of the Dutch East Indies, using the Australian First Army for the ground operations. Operating from the Philippines, I could sweep down on these Japanese held islands from the rear.

I spoke of my esteem for Admiral King and his wise estimate of the importance of the Pacific as a major element in the global picture, however I might disagree with some of his strategic concepts.

Admiral Leahy seemed to support what I said, and the President accepted my recommendations and approved the Philippine plan.

Through the understanding assistance of our Navy, I was able to send in by submarine—in driblets at first—arms, ammunition, and medical supplies. News of the first such shipment spread rapidly by the "bamboo telegraph" through the Philippines to electrify the people into full returning consciousness that America had neither abandoned nor forgotten them.

Later, as resources increased, I was able, after formalizing the guerrilla forces by their recognition and incorporation into units of our army, to send through Philippine coastal contacts vitally needed supplies in ever-increasing quantities, by four submarines committed exclusively to that purpose.

The story of the resistance of the people of the Philippines to the Japanese occupation of their land is a saga of unflinching devotion to those

Above:
With Brigadier General
Ennis P. Whitehead.

Below:
Leaving Australia
for New Guinea.

Facing page:
With the troops—New Guinea.

precepts of freedom inculcated into their hearts during forty years under the American flag, of an indomitable will to hold aloft the torch of human liberty when little hope seemed left for its survival, of a militant and unflagging loyalty to the United States and the American people.

There is probably no better expression of this devotion and loyalty and will than is contained in the letters of two patriots from widely separated parts of the archipelago which were circulated throughout the land, copies of which I received by submarine in the early fall of 1943. The one from Governor Thomas Confessor, a Christian Filipino political leader, was in reply to a letter from Dr. Fermin Caram which urged him to collaborate with the Japanese. It was dated February 20, 1943, and read in part:

This struggle is a total war in which the issues between the warring parties are less concerned with territorial questions but more with forms of government, ways of life, and things that affect even the very thought, feelings and sentiments of every man. In other words, the question at stake with respect to the Philippines is not whether Japan or the U.S. should possess it but fundamentally it is: what system of government should stand here and what ways of life; what system of social organization and code for morals should govern our existence.

The burden of your so-called message to me consists of the entreaty that further bloodshed and destruction of property in Panay should stop and that our people be saved from further suffering and misery resulting from warfare and hostilities now existing between Japan and ourselves. The responsibility, however, of accomplishing this end does not rest upon us but entirely upon your friends who have sworn allegiance to Japan. For it was Japan that projected and created those conditions; Japan is the sole author of the holocaust in the Far East.

You may not agree with me but the truth is that the present war is a blessing in disguise to our people and that the burden it imposes and the hardships it has brought upon us are a test of our character to determine the sincerity of our convictions and the integrity of our souls. In other words, this war has placed us in the crucible to assay the metal in our being. For as a people, we have been living during the last 40 years under a regime of justice and liberty regulated only by universally accepted principles of constitutional government. We have come to enjoy personal privileges and civil liberties without much struggle, without undergoing any pain to attain them. They were practically a gift from a generous and magnanimous people—the people of the United States of America.

Now that Japan is attempting to destroy those liberties, should we not exert any effort to defend them? Should we not be willing to suffer for their defense? If our people are undergoing hardships now, we are doing it gladly; it is because we are willing to pay the price for those constitutional liberties and privileges. You cannot become wealthy by honest means without sweating heavily. You very well know that the principles of democracy and democratic institutions were brought to life through bloodshed and fire. If we sincerely believe in those principles and institutions, as we who are resisting Japan do, we should contribute to the utmost of our capacity to the cost of its maintenance to save them from destruction and annihilation, and such contribution should be in terms of painful sacrifice, the same currency that other peoples paid for these principles. . . .

You are decidedly wrong when you tell me that there is no ignominy in surrender. That may be true in the case of soldiers who were corralled by the enemy consisting of superior force, with no way of escape whatsoever. For when they gave themselves up they did not repudiate any principle of good government or of life which inspired them to fight heroically and valiantly—to use your own words. Should I surrender, however, and with me the people, by your own invitation and assurance of guarantee to my life, my family and those who follow me, I should be surrendering something more precious than life itself: the principles of democracy and justice, and the honor and destiny of our people.

I note you emphasized in your letter only peace and the tranquility of our people. I do not know whether by omission or intentionally you failed to refer in any way to the honor and destiny of our race. You seem to have forgotten those noble sentiments already, despite the fact that Japan has hardly been a year in our country. It appears clearly evident, therefore, that there is a great difference between the manner in which we are trying to lead our people during these trying days. You and your fellow puppets are trying to give them peace and tranquility by destroying their dignity and honor, without suffering, or if there is any, the least possible. On the other hand, we endeavor to inspire them to face difficulties and undergo any sacrifice to uphold the noble principles of popular rule and constitutional government, thereby holding up high and immaculate their honor and dignity at the same time. . . .

You may have read, I am sure, the story of Lincoln who held firmly to the conviction that the secession of the southern states from the northern was wrong. Consequently, when he became the President and the southern states seceded he did not hesitate to use force to compel them to remain in the union. The immediate result was civil war that involved the country in the throes of a terrible armed conflict that, according to reliable historians, produced proportion-

Above:
Milne Bay. With
General Krueger.

Facing page, top row and middle:
With the troops—New Guinea.
"A stinking jungle of twisted,
slime-covered roots and muddy soup.
After a man had lain for days
in a wet slit trench, or in the swamp,
his physical stamina was reduced materially.
The unfamiliar noises of the jungle,
spectors of Japanese activities, preyed
on his mind until he was reduced often
to a pitifully abject state
incapable of aggressive action."

Facing page, bottom:
MacArthur and Marine Major General
W. H. Rupertus on inspection tour
in Southwest Pacific

Right top: Port Moresby.

Right bottom:
Somewhere in the South Pacific.

Above:
New Britain.

Facing page:
Borneo campaign.

Below:
Discussing plans for
aerial attack on Lae
with Colonel Tolson.

Following page:
Allied troops in action in New Caledonia.

ately more loss of lives, hardships and miseries than the First World War. The sufferings of the people of the south were terrible but the union was saved and America has become thereby one of the strongest and most respected nations on the surface of the earth. If Lincoln had revised his convictions and sacrificed them for the sake of peace and tranquility as you did, a fatal catastrophe would have befallen the people of America. With this lesson of history clearly before us, I prefer to follow Lincoln's example than yours and your fellow puppets. . . .

I will not surrender as long as I can stand on my feet. The people may suffer now and may suffer more during the next months. To use the words of St. Paul the Apostle: "The sufferings of the present are not worthy to be compared with the glory to come that shall be revealed in us."

The other letter was from Datu Manaleo Mindalano, a Moro leader of the Mohammedan faith, in answer to an attempt by Captain K. Takemoto, local Japanese commander, to induce him to collaborate. It was dated July 3, 1943, and read in part:

It gives me no surprise to hear from you Japanese the same old alibi that you came to the Philippines with good intentions. What have you done in Lanao that is worth appreciating anyway? When you came, you kill the natives like chicken and attack towns and barrios who are innocent. Now that you cannot force us to submission and your doomsday is in sight, your note is sorrowful. . . .

You can be very sure that I will continue to redouble my efforts in attacking places wherever I smell Japs. If I have been active when I was fighting by my own accord, you should expect a much more terrific attack from me now that I am following military orders and have taken oath reaffirming my allegiance to the Commonwealth of the Philippines and the United States of America. . . . If I were to choose between being a pro-satan and pro-Japanese, I would choose being the former just to be always against Japanism of all types in the Philippines. Had you been enlightened enough in the affairs, the psychology, the needs, and well-being of my people, the Maranaos, you would not keep on wondering why I will never be tempted by your persuasive propaganda and sugarcoated promises and why, in spite of a temporary collapse of U.S. Army resistance in the country on account of the surrender of the main USAFFE Forces in the Philippines, I have not only withstood the defense of my sector but have continued harassing your forces wherever we met until you became imprisoned in the fox holes of your garrisons. . . .

Believe me, if there is any impossibility under the sun, it is a Philippine Independence granted by Japan. . . . Before this war, America promised the Philippines her independence in 1946. We honor

Above and preceding page:
Preparing for the invasion
of the Philippines. With President Roosevelt,
Admiral Chester W. Nimitz, and
Admiral William D. Leahy. Hawaii, 1944.

American promises after a close observation of their character for over 40 years. But Japan's one-year commitment does not warrant honoring her promise of independence even if the date of that promise were to take effect tomorrow.

Receipt of these letters filled me with a sense of deep pride and infinite assurance in the ultimate triumph of the cause of Philippine liberation. For they reflected a spirit of dynamic patriotism unexcelled by any patriots of any age. They gave me the measure of the internal support I might expect when the lines of battle converged on Philippine soil.

I had no illusions about the operation. I knew it was to be the crucial battle of the war in the Pacific. On its outcome would depend the fate of the Philippines and the future of the war against Japan. Leyte was to be the anvil against which I hoped to hammer the Japanese into submission in the central Philippines—the springboard from which I could proceed to the conquest of Luzon, for the final assault against Japan itself. With the initiative in my hands, the war had reached that decisive stage where an important Japanese defeat would seal the fate of the Japanese Empire and a centuries-old tradition of invincibility.

On October 16th, I left Hollandia and went aboard the *Nashville*, which was to serve as my flagship. On the waters around me lay one of the greatest armadas of history. America's rebuilt strength consisted of new battleships that replaced those lying at the bottom of Pearl Harbor, and many of the veteran ships that had survived that initial assault itself; of aircraft carriers, cruisers, and destroyers in massive array; of transports and landing craft of a type that had not even existed three years before. Altogether, there were 700 of these ships of war. They carried 174,000 of America's finest fighting men, veteran soldiers now a match for any warrior the world has ever known. The size of the landing force was equal to about half the Japanese strength in the islands, but the enemy was scattered. My force was concentrated. I intended my maneuver and surprise to bring a superior force to bear at the points of actual combat and, thereby, to destroy him piecemeal.

It is difficult even for one who was there to adequately describe the scene of the next two days. Ships to the front, to the rear, to the left, and to the right, as far as the eye could see. Their sturdy hulls plowed the water, now presenting a broadside view, now their sterns, as they methodically carried out the zigzag tactics of evasion.

We came to Leyte just before midnight of a dark and moonless night. The stygian waters below and the black sky above seemed to conspire in wrapping us in an invisible cloak, as we lay to and waited for dawn before entering Leyte Gulf. Phase one of the plan had been accomplished with little resistance. Now and then a ghostly ship would slide quietly by us, looming out of the night and disappearing into the gloom almost before its outlines could be depicted. I knew that on every ship nervous men lined the rails or paced the decks, peering into the darkness and wondering what stood out there beyond the night waiting for the dawn to come. There is a universal sameness in the emotions of men, whether they be admiral or sailor, general or private, at such a time as this. On almost every ship one could count on seeing groups huddled around maps in the wardrooms, infantrymen nervously inspecting their rifles, the crews of the ships testing their gear, last-minute letters being written, men with special missions or objectives trying to visualize them again. For every man there were tons of supplies and equipment—trucks and vehicles of all kinds, and more than one ton of ammunition for every man who would storm those shores. Late that evening I went back to my cabin and read again those passages from the Bible from which I have always gained inspiration and hope. And I prayed that a merciful God would preserve each one of those men on the morrow.

The big guns on the ships opened fire at dawn. The noise, like rolling thunder, was all around us. The *Nashville,* her engines bringing to life the steel under our feet, knifed into Leyte Gulf. The ominous clouds of night still hung over the sea, fighting the sun for possession of the sky, but the blackness had given way to somber gray, and even as we saw the black outline of the shore on the horizon, the cloak of drabness began to roll back. On every side ships were riding toward the island. The battle for Leyte had already begun.

I was on the bridge with Captain C. E. Coney. His clear, keen eyes and cool, crisp voice swung the cruiser first to port, then to starboard as he dodged floating mines. An enemy periscope suddenly spouted up, only to be blotted out as destroyers closed in with roaring depth charges. And then, just as the sun rose clear of the horizon, there was Tacloban. It had changed little since I had known it forty-one years before on my first assignment after leaving West Point. It was a full moment for me.

The invasion of the Philippines.

Above:
The invasion of Leyte.
"Red Beach."

Facing page, top:
Greeting Rear Admiral
Daniel A. Berbey.

Shortly after this, we reached our appointed position offshore. The captain carefully hove into line and dropped anchor. Our initial vantage point was 2 miles from the beaches, but I could clearly see the sandstrips with the pounding surf beating down upon the shore, and in the morning sunlight, the jungle-clad hills rising behind the town. Landings are explosive once the shooting begins, and now thousands of guns were throwing their shells with a roar that was incessant and deafening. Rocket vapor trails crisscrossed the sky and black, ugly, ominous pillars of smoke began to rise. High overhead, swarms of airplanes darted into the maelstrom. And across what would ordinarily have been a glinting, untroubled blue sea, the black dots of the landing craft churned toward the beaches.

From my vantage point, I had a clear view of everything that took place. Troops were going ashore at "Red Beach," near Palo, at San Jose on "White Beach" and at the southern tip of Leyte on tiny Panson Island. On the north, under Major General Franklin C. Sibert, the X Corps, made up of the 1st Cavalry and 24th Infantry Divisions; to the south, the XXIV Corps, under Major General John R. Hodge, consisting of the 7th and 96th Infantry Divisions. In over-all command of ground troops was Lieutenant General Walter Kreuger of the Sixth Army.

At "Red Beach" our troops secured a landing and began moving inland. I decided to go in with the third assault wave. President Osmena, accompanied by General Basilio Valdez, the Philippine Army chief of staff, and General Carlos Romulo, my old aide, who had joined me on Bataan in 1942, had sailed with the convoy on one of the nearby transports. I took them into my landing barge and we started for the beach. Romulo, an old stalwart of the Quezon camp, was the resident commissioner for the Philippines in Washington. Noted for his oratorical ability, this popular patriot served on Bataan, and had been the radio "Voice of Freedom" from Corregidor.

As we slowly bucked the waves toward "Red Beach," the sounds of war grew louder. We could now hear the whining roar of airplane engines as they dove over our heads to strafe and bomb enemy positions inland from the beach. Then came the steady crump, crump of exploding naval shells. As we came closer, we could pick up the shouts of our soldiers as they gave and acknowledged orders. Then, unmistakably, in the near dis-

Facing page:
"People of the Philippines:
I have returned."

Following pages:
"As I dropped off to sleep
the vision that danced before
my tired eyes was not of bullet,
bayonet or bomb, but of
an old, old man, a resident of Leyte,
who stepped up to me
amidst the shock and shell
of the afternoon, welcoming me with
outstretched arms. 'Good afternoon,
Sir Field Marshal. Glad to see you.
It has been many years—
a long, long time.' "

Above and below:
Shortly after landing
on Leyte, MacArthur
confers with President
Sergio Osmena.

Facing page:
The man who came back.

tance came the steady rattle of small-arms fire. I could easily pick up the peculiar fuzzy gurgle of a Japanese machine gun seemingly not more than 100 yards from the shoreline. The smoke from the burning palm trees was in our nostrils, and we could hear the continual snapping and crackling of flames. The coxswain dropped the ramp about 50 yards from shore, and we waded in. It took me only 30 or 40 long strides to reach dry land, but that was one of the most meaningful walks I ever took. When it was done, and I stood on the sand, I knew I was back again—against my old enemies of Bataan, for there, shining on the bodies of dead Japanese soldiers, I saw the insignia of the 16th Division, General Homma's ace unit.

Our beachhead troops were only a few yards away, stretched out behind logs and other cover, laying down fire on the area immediately inland. There were still Japanese in the undergrowth not many yards away. A mobile broadcasting unit was set up, and as I got ready to talk into the microphone, the rains came down. This is what I said:

People of the Philippines: I have returned. By the grace of Almighty God, our forces stand again on Philippine soil—soil consecrated in the blood of our two peoples. We have come, dedicated and committed to the task of destroying every vestige of enemy control over your daily lives, and of restoring upon a foundation of indestructible strength, the liberties of your people.

At my side is your President, Sergio Osmena, a worthy successor of that great patriot, Manuel Quezon, with members of his cabinet. The seat of your government is now, therefore, firmly re-established on Philippine soil.

The hour of your redemption is here. Your patriots have demonstrated an unswerving and resolute devotion to the principles of freedom that challenge the best that is written on the pages of human history. I now call upon your supreme effort that the enemy may know, from the temper of an aroused people within, that he has a force there to contend with no less violent than is the force committed from without.

Rally to me. Let the indomitable spirit of Bataan and Corregidor lead on. As the lines of battle roll forward to bring you within the zone of operations, rise and strike. Strike at every favorable opportunity. For your homes and hearths, strike! For future generations of your sons and daughters, strike! In the name of your sacred dead, strike! Let no heart be faint. Let every arm be steeled. The guidance of Divine God points the way. Follow in His name to the Holy Grail of righteous victory.

President Osmena and I then walked off the

beach, and picked our way into the brush behind the beach until we found a place to sit down. We had made our return and it was time to think of returning the government to constitutional authority. It was while we were finishing our discussion that the beachhead was subjected for the first time to an enemy bombing attack. It shook the log on which we sat, but that was all. As we finally got up to move, I noticed that the rain was no longer falling and that the only soldiers left near the beach were members of sniper patrols.

I wrote the following letter to President Roosevelt:

> Near Tacloban, Philippine Islands
> October 20, 1944
>
> Dear Mr. President:
>
> This note is written from the beach near Tacloban where we have just landed. It will be the first letter from the freed Philippines. I thought you might like it for your philatelic collection. I hope it gets through.
>
> The operation is going smoothly and if successful will strategically as well as tactically cut the enemy forces in two. Strategically it will pierce the center of his defensive line extending along the coast of Asia from the Japanese homeland to the tip of Singapore, and will enable us to envelop to the north or south as we desire. It severs completely the Japanese from their infamous propaganda slogan of the "Greater East Asia Co-Prosperity Sphere." Tactically it divides his forces in the Philippines in two and by by-passing the southern half of the Philippines will result in the saving of possibly fifty thousand American casualties. He had expected us and prepared on Mindanao.
>
> The Filipinos are reacting splendidly and I feel that a successful campaign of liberation if promptly followed by a dramatic granting to them of independence will place American prestige in the Far East at the highest pinnacle of all times.
>
> Once more, on the highest plane of statesmanship, I venture to urge that this great ceremony be presided over by you in person. Such a step will electrify the world and redound immeasurably to the credit and honor of the United States for a thousand years.
>
> Please excuse this scribble but at the moment I am on the combat line with no facilities except this field message pad.
>
> Very faithfully

After inspecting the forward elements of our troops and the Tacloban Airfield, I returned to the *Nashville*. That evening I ordered a co-ordinated attack by guerrillas all over the Philippines.

As I dropped off to sleep that night, the vision that danced before my tired eyes was not of bayonet, bullet, or bomb, but of an old, old man, a resi-

Facing page, top:
Rangers wounded on Luzon.

Facing page, bottom:
Lieutenant General Walter Krueger and MacArthur meet after effectuating a division of the Japanese forces in the Philippines.

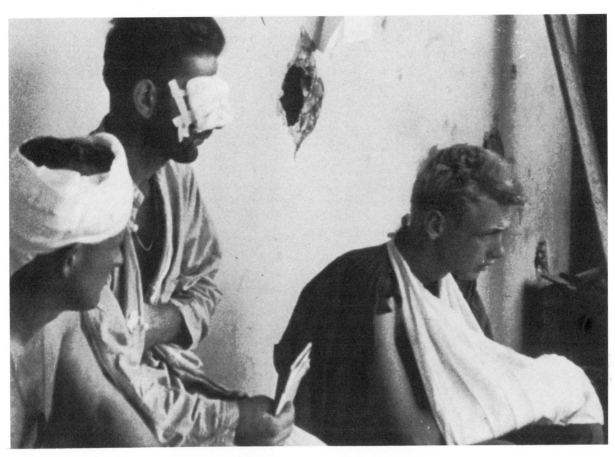

dent of Leyte, who stepped up to me amidst the shot and shell of the afternoon, welcoming me with outstretched arms. "Good afternoon, Sir Field Marshal," he said in his Visayan dialect. "Glad to see you. It has been many years—a long, long time."

As the end of the Philippine campaign approached, plans were considered regarding the future of the war. Captured documents revealed a fatal degree of exhaustion of Japan's heavy and armament industries. It was known that the Japanese ambassador to Moscow was making frantic appeals to the Soviet Foreign minister to have Russia intercede as a neutral in developing a basis for an armistice and peace with the United States.

Toward the end of 1944 and in early 1945 the question of Russian intervention in the Pacific was seriously considered in such international discussions as Yalta. The political, economic and military effect of such intervention seemed to have become a vital factor in those secret understandings. From my viewpoint, any intervention by Russia during 1945 was not required.

Above, below and facing page: A hero's return.

On July 26th, 1945,

came the Potsdam ultimatum giving Japan the single choice of surrender or destruction. The Japanese government failed to accept promptly the terms of the Potsdam proclamation, and as a direct consequence Japan became the victim of the most destructive and revolutionary weapon in the long history of warfare—the atom bomb. The first bomb of this type ever used against an enemy was released early on August 6th from an American Superfortress over the military base city of Hiroshima, and exploded with incomparable and devastating force. The city was almost completely and uniformly leveled. The development of nuclear weapons had not been revealed to me until just prior to the attack on Hiroshima.

On August 7th, President Truman shook the world with a broadcast statement which declared:

Sixteen hours ago an American airplane dropped one bomb on Hiroshima, an important Japanese army base. This bomb had more power than 20,000 tons of TNT. With this bomb we have now added a new and revolutionary increase in destruction to supplement the growing power of our armed forces. It is an atomic bomb. It is a harnessing of the basic power of the universe. We are now prepared to obliterate more rapidly and completely every productive enterprise

Above and right:
A hero's return.

Facing page, top:
Restoration of the
government of the
Philippines.

Facing page, bottom:
Visiting Bilibid Prison
in Manila, site of
Japanese internment camp.

the Japanese have above ground in any city. We shall destroy their docks, their factories, and their communications. Let there be no mistake; we shall completely destroy Japan's power to make war. It was to spare the Japanese people from utter destruction that the ultimatum of July 26 was issued at Potsdam.

On August 8th, with the world still reeling from this shattering experience, the Soviet Union formally declared war on Japan—following four years of pretentious neutrality that had allowed Japanese forces to move against and occupy New Guinea and the Philippines, instead of being tied down to guarding the Siberian frontier. The Russians attacked the Japanese Kwangtung Army in Manchuria and sent a military mission to my headquarters in Manila. It was headed by General Kuzma Derevyanko, an officer of considerable ability who later became the Soviet diplomatic representative in Tokyo.

On August 9th, a second atomic bomb destroyed the city of Nagasaki amid a cloud of dust and debris that rose 50,000 feet and was visible for more than 175 miles. The two bombs which fell on Hiroshima and Nagasaki were dropped by the 509th Composite Bomb Group based on Tinian and belonging to General Arnold's strategic command. The selection of Nagasaki as the second objective of the atomic bomb was caused by unfavorable weather conditions. After circling for fifty minutes above the smoke-obscured city of Kokura, which was the primary target, the bombing plane flew on to drop the bomb over Nagasaki, the alternate target. Kokura was spared by a blind miracle of chance, but in Nagasaki 100,000 inhabitants died within seconds.

By August 10th, Japan had had enough. After much internal struggle and argument, the Japanese government instructed its minister to Switzerland to advise the United States through the Swiss government that the terms of the Potsdam ultimatum would be accepted if Japan's national polity could be preserved. The Japanese note read in part:

The Japanese Government several weeks ago asked the Soviet Government, with which neutral relations then prevailed, to render good offices in restoring peace vis-a-vis the enemy power. Unfortunately, these efforts in the interest of peace having failed, the Japanese Government in conformity with the august wish of His Majesty to restore the general peace, and desiring to put an end to the untold sufferings entailed by war as soon as possible, have decided upon the following:

The Japanese Government are ready to accept the terms enumerated in the joint declaration which was issued at Potsdam on July 26th, 1945, by the heads of the Governments of the United States, Great Britain, and China, and later subscribed to by the Soviet Government with the understanding that the said declaration does not comprise any demand which prejudices the prerogatives of His Majesty as a Sovereign Ruler.

The Japanese Government sincerely hope that this understanding is warranted and desire keenly that an explicit indication to that effect will be speedily forthcoming.

On August 11th, the United States, acting on behalf of the United Nations, transmitted a reply which stated:

From the moment of surrender the authority of the Emperor and the Japanese Government to rule the state shall be subject to the Supreme Commander of the Allied Powers who will take such steps as he deems proper to effectuate the surrender terms.

The Emperor will be required to authorize and ensure the signature by the Government of Japan and the Japanese Imperial General Headquarters of the surrender terms necessary to carry out the provisions of the Potsdam Declaration, and shall issue his commands to all the Japanese military, naval, and air authorities and to all the forces under their control wherever located to cease active operations and to surrender their arms, and to issue such other orders as the Supreme Commander may require to give effect to the surrender terms.

Immediately upon the surrender, the Japanese Government shall transport prisoners of war and civilian internees to places of safety as directed, where they can quickly be placed aboard Allied transports.

The ultimate form of government of Japan shall, in accordance with the Potsdam Declaration, be established by the freely expressed will of the Japanese people.

The armed forces of the Allied Powers will remain in Japan until the purposes set forth in the Potsdam Declaration are achieved.

While the Japanese government pondered the Allied answer, President Truman, on August 12th, directed the strategic air force to cease its attacks. The Far East air forces of my command and the Allied fleet in Japanese waters continued their steady pounding. When no reply was received from the Japanese by August 13th, the strategic air force was ordered to renew its operations and on the same day 1,000 carrier planes from Halsey's Third Fleet made their final raid on Tokyo.

Never before in history had one nation been

Above and below:
Arriving at Corregidor.

Following pages:
Return to "Topside."

the target of such concentrated air power. In the last fifteen days of the war, my Fifth and Seventh Air Forces flew 6,372 sorties against Kyushu alone. Thus, with a deafening roar of blasting bombs, Kenney's Far East air forces culminated their blows against Japan. During the last seven and a half months of the war, their planes destroyed 2,846,932 tons of shipping and 1,375 enemy aircraft, dropped 100,000 tons of bombs, and flew over 150,000 sorties.

The 15th of August was an eventful date in history: Japan's notification of final surrender was received in the United States; President Truman announced the end of conflict in the Pacific; the Emperor of Japan made a dramatic and unparalleled broadcast to his people announcing the surrender. It was a notable day for me, too—I was made Supreme Commander for the Allied Powers.

Left:
On arrival at Atsugi
Airport in Japan.

Facing page, top:
"From my viewpoint,
any intervention by Russia
during 1945 was not required."

Facing page, bottom:
Manila, 1945.

Part IV

Occupation of Japan

September 2, 1945,

was fixed for the formal ceremonies of surrender
aboard the *Missouri*. I did not participate in the
original negotiations for the surrender, but after
the Japanese government had agreed to terms, the
task of implementation fell to me. I had received
no instructions as to what to say or what to do. I
was on my own, standing on the quarterdeck with
only God and my own conscience to guide me.

My favorite account of what occurred and
what was said that morning was one officially
rendered to the Emperor by Mr. Toshikazu Kase,
a member of the Japanese surrender party.

It was a surprisingly cool day for early September.
The sky was dull gray with clouds hanging low. We
left Tokyo at about five o'clock in the morning. There
were nine of us, three each from the Foreign Office,
and the War and Navy Departments, besides the two
delegates, Shigemitsu, the Foreign Minister representing the government, and General Umedzu, the Chief
of Staff of the Army representing the Supreme Command. With the two delegates leading the procession,
our cars sped at full speed on the battered and bumpy
road to Yokohama. Along the highway, we could see
nothing but miles and miles of debris and destruction
where there had once flourished towns containing a
great number of munitions factories. The ghastly
sight of death and desolation was enough to freeze
my heart. These hollow ruins, however, were perhaps
a fit prelude to the poignant drama in which we were
about to take part for were we not sorrowing men
come to seek a tomb for a fallen Empire? They were
also a grim reminder that a nation was snatched from
an impending annihilation. For were not the scenes
of havoc the atomic bomb wrought a sufficient warning? The waste of war and the ignominy of surrender
were put on my mental loom and produced a strange
fabric of grief and sorrow. There were few men on
the road and none probably recognized us. Our journey was kept in utmost secrecy in order to avoid
publicity lest extremists might attempt to impede us
by violence.

To begin with, there was much ado in selecting

the delegates. Nobody wanted to volunteer for the odious duty. The Prime Minister, Prince Higashikuni, was the Emperor's uncle and was considered unsuitable on that account. Next choice fell on Prince Konoye, who was Vice Premier and the real power in the government, but he shunned the ordeal. Finally the mission was assigned to Shigemitsu, the Foreign Minister. On accepting the imperial command to sign the surrender document as principal delegate, he confided to me what an honor he felt it, since it was the mark of the sovereign's confidence in him. Shigemitsu, who had served twice before as Foreign Minister—namely, in the latter period of the Tojo Cabinet and through the duration of the succeeding Koiso Cabinet—is a man of confirmed peaceful views and during his twelve months' term of office did his utmost to prepare for an early termination of the war. His efforts, in which I assisted him to the best of my ability, were in fact, powerfully instrumental in expediting the restoration of peace. Such being the case, there was reason to believe that unlike others who evaded the mission, hating it as unbearably onerous, Shigemitsu regarded it as a painful but profitable task. In his mind he was determined to make this day of national mortification the starting point for a renewed pilgrimage onward toward the goal, though dim and distant, of a peaceful state. If this day marked a journey's end it must also signify a journey's beginning. Only the traveler to grief must be replaced by the traveler to glory.

Not so with General Umedzu, who reluctantly accepted the appointment as the second delegate. He had opposed the termination of hostilities to the last moment and was, moreover, a soldier born to command and not to sue. When he was recommended for the mission he grew, so it is reported, pale with anger and laconically remarked that if it was forced upon him, he would instantly commit hara-kiri in protest. It required the Emperor's personal persuasion to make him execute the duties with good grace.

It may sound somewhat silly, but as precautions were then deemed necessary, the appointment of two delegates was not intimated to the press until the last moment. The names of nine persons who accompanied them were not published at all as the service officers were against this, though these names had been communicated to and approved by the Allied authorities. Such, indeed, was the temper of the times.

This party arrived in Yokohama in less than an hour's time. It was on this day that the spearhead of the Eighth Army landed at the same port. Sentries with gleaming bayonets were heavily guarding the streets through which we rode slowly to the port area. All the cars had removed the flags on the bonnet and officers had left their swords behind, at the office of the Prefectural Governor where we rested a while. We had thus furled the banner and ungirt the sword. Diplomats without flag and soldiers without sword—sullen

Facing page:
Surrender ceremonies aboard
the battleship *Missouri.*
"A new era is upon us.
Even the lesson of victory itself
brings with it a profound concern
both for our future security and
the survival of civilization."

and silent we continued the journey till we reached the quay.

There were four destroyers with white placards hung on the mast marked A to D. We boarded the one marked B, which was the *Lansdown,* a ship which saw much meritorious service in the battle of the Pacific. As the destroyer pushed out of the harbor, we saw in the offing lines on lines of gray warships, both heavy and light, anchored in majestic array. This was the mighty pageant of the Allied navies that so lately belched forth their crashing battle, now holding in their swift thunder and floating like calm sea birds on the subjugated waters. A spirit of gay festivity pervaded the atmosphere.

After about an hour's cruise the destroyer stopped in full view of the battleship *Missouri,* which lay anchored some eighteen miles off the shore. The huge 45,000 tonner towered high above the rest of the proud squadron. High on the mast there fluttered in the wind the Stars and Stripes. It was this flag that has lighted the marching step of America's destiny on to shining victory. Today this flag of glory was raised in triumph to mark the Big Day. As we approached the battleship in a motor launch, our eyes were caught by rows of sailors massed on her broadside lining the rails, a starry multitude, in their glittering uniforms of immaculate white.

Soon the launch came alongside the battleship, and we climbed its gangway, Shigemitsu leading the way, heavily limping on his cane. For he walks on a wooden leg, having had his leg blown off by a bomb outrage in Shanghai some fifteen years ago. It was as if he negotiated each step with a groan and we, the rest of us, echoed it with a sigh. As we, eleven in all, climbed onto the veranda deck on the starboard side, we gathered into three short rows facing the representatives of the Allied powers across a table covered with green cloth, on which were placed the white documents of surrender. The veranda deck was animated by a motley of sparkling colors, red, gold, brown, and olive, as decorations and ribbons decked the uniforms of different cut and color worn by the Allied representatives. There were also row upon row of American admirals and generals in somber khaki; but what added to the festive gayety of the occasion was the sight of the war correspondents who, monkey-like, hung on to every cliff-like point of vantage in most precarious postures. Evidently scaffolding had been specially constructed for the convenience of the cameramen, who were working frantically on their exciting job. Then there was a gallery of spectators who seemed numberless, overcrowding every bit of available space on the great ship, on the mast, on the chimneys, on the gun turrets—on everything and everywhere.

They were all thronged, packed to suffocation, representatives, journalists, spectators, an assembly of brass, braid, and brand. As we appeared on the scene we were, I felt, being subjected to the torture of the pillory. There were a million eyes beating us in the million shafts of a rattling storm of arrows barbed with fire. I felt their keenness sink into my body with a sharp physical pain. Never have I realized that the glance of glaring eyes could hurt so much.

We waited for a few minutes standing in the public gaze like penitent boys awaiting the dreaded schoolmaster. I tried to preserve with the utmost sangfroid the dignity of defeat, but it was difficult and every minute seemed to contain ages. I looked up and saw painted on the wall nearby several miniature Rising Suns, our flag, evidently in numbers corresponding to the planes and submarines shot down or sunk by the crew of the battleship. As I tried to count these markings, tears rose in my throat and quickly gathered to the eyes, flooding them. I could hardly bear the sight now. Heroes of unwritten stories, they were young boys who defied death gaily and gallantly, manning the daily thinning ranks of the suicide corps. They were just like cherry blossoms, emblems of our national character, all of a sudden blooming into riotous beauty and just as quickly going away. What do they see today, their spirit, the glorious thing, looking down on the scene of our surrender?

MacArthur walks quietly from the interior of the ship and steps to the microphones:

"We are gathered here, representatives of the major warring powers," he said, "to conclude a solemn agreement whereby peace may be restored. The issues, involving divergent ideals and ideologies, have been determined on the battlefields of the world and hence are not for our discussion or debate. Nor is it for us here to meet, representing as we do a majority of the people of the earth, in a spirit of distrust, malice or hatred. But rather it is for us, both victors and vanquished, to rise to that higher dignity which alone befits the sacred purposes we are about to serve, committing all our people unreservedly to faithful compliance with the obligation they are here formally to assume.

"It is my earnest hope and indeed the hope of all mankind that from this solemn occasion a better world shall emerge out of the blood and carnage of the past—a world founded upon faith and understanding—a world dedicated to the dignity of man and the fulfillment of his most cherished wish—for freedom, tolerance and justice.

"The terms and conditions upon which the surrender of the Japanese Imperial Forces is here to be given and accepted are contained in the instrument of surrender now before you.

"As Supreme Commander for the Allied Powers, I announce it my firm purpose, in the tradition of the countries I represent, to proceed in the discharge of my responsibilities with justice and tolerance, while taking all necessary dispositions to insure that the terms of surrender are fully, promptly and faithfully complied with."

In a few minutes' time the speech was over and the Supreme Commander invited the Japanese delegates to sign the instrument of surrender. Shigemitsu signed first followed by Umedzu. It was eight minutes past nine when MacArthur put his signature to the documents. Other representatives of the Allied Powers followed suit in the order of the United States, China, the United Kingdom, the Soviet Union, Australia, Canada, France, the Netherlands and New Zealand.

When all the representatives had finished signing, MacArthur announced slowly: "Let us pray that peace be now restored to the world and that God will preserve it always. These proceedings are closed."

At that moment, the skies parted and the sun shone brightly through the layers of clouds. There was a steady drone above and now it became a deafening roar and an armada of airplanes paraded into sight, sweeping over the warships. Four hundred B-29's and 1,500 carrier planes joined in the aerial pageant in a final salute. It was over.

MacArthur broadcast to the American people:

"Today the guns are silent. A great tragedy has ended. A great victory has been won. The skies no longer rain death—the seas bear only commerce—men everywhere walk upright in the sunlight. The entire world is quietly at peace. The holy mission has been completed. And in reporting this to you, the people, I speak for the thousands of silent lips, forever stilled among the jungles and the beaches and in the deep waters of the Pacific which marked the way. I speak for the unnamed brave millions homeward bound to take up the challenge of that future which they did so much to salvage from the brink of disaster.

"As I look back on the long, tortuous trail from those grim days of Bataan and Corregidor, when an entire world lived in fear, when democracy was on the defensive everywhere, when modern civilization trembled in the balance, I thank a merciful God that He has given us the faith, the courage and the power from which to mould victory. We have known the bitterness of defeat and the exultation of triumph, and from both we have learned there can be no turning back. We must go forward to preserve in peace what we won in war.

"A new era is upon is. Even the lesson of victory itself brings with it profound concern, both for our future security and the survival of civilization. The destructiveness of the war potential, through progressive advances in scientific discovery, has in fact now reached a point which revises the traditional concept of war.

"Men since the beginning of time have sought peace. Various methods through the ages have attempted to devise an international process to prevent or settle disputes between nations. From the very start workable methods were found insofar as individual citizens were concerned, but the mechanics of an instrumentality of larger international scope have never been successful. Military alliances, balances of power, leagues of nations, all in turn failed, leaving the only path to be by way of the crucible of war. We have had our last chance. If we do not now devise some greater and more equitable system, Armageddon will be at our door. The problem basically is theological and involves a spiritual recrudescence and improvement of human character that will synchronize with our almost matchless advances in science, art, literature and all material and cultural developments of the past two thousand years. It must be of the spirit if we are to save the flesh.

"We stand in Tokyo today reminiscent of our countryman, Commodore Perry, ninety-two years ago. His purpose was to bring to Japan an era of enlightenment and progress, by lifting the veil of isolation to the friendship, trade, and commerce of the world. But, alas, the knowledge thereby gained of Western science was forged into an instrument of oppression and human enslavement. Freedom of expression, freedom of action, even freedom of thought were denied through appeal to superstition, and through the application of force. We are committed by the Potsdam Declaration of principles to see that the Japanese people are liberated from this condition of slavery. It is my purpose to implement this commitment just as rapidly as the armed forces are demobilized and other essential steps taken to neutralize the war potential.

"The energy of the Japanese race, if properly directed, will enable expansion vertically rather than horizontally. If the talents of the race are turned into constructive channels, the country can lift itself from its present deplorable state into a position of dignity.

"To the Pacific basin has come the vista of a new emancipated world. Today, freedom is on the offensive, democracy is on the march. Today, in Asia as well as in Europe, unshackled peoples are tasting the full sweetness of liberty, the relief from fear.

"In the Philippines, America has evolved a model for this new free world of Asia. In the Philippines, America has demonstrated that peoples of the East and peoples of the West may walk side by side in mutual respect and with mutual benefit. The history of our sovereignty there has now the full confidence of the East.

"And so, my fellow countrymen, today I report to you that your sons and daughters have served you well and faithfully with the calm, deliberate, determined fighting spirit of the American soldier and sailor, based upon a tradition of historical truth as against the fanaticism of an enemy supported only by

mythological fiction. Their spiritual strength and power has brought us through to victory. They are homeward bound—take care of them."

When the Supreme Commander finished, I wrote in my report the impression his words had made on me. He is a man of peace. Never has the truth of the line "peace has her victories no less renowned than war" been more eloquently demonstrated. He is a man of light. Radiantly, the gathering rays of his magnanimous soul embrace the earth, his footsteps paving the world with light. Is it not a piece of rare good fortune, I asked myself, that a man of such caliber and character should have been designated as the Supreme Commander who will shape the destiny of Japan? In the dark hour of our despair and distress, a bright light is ushered in, in the very person of General MacArthur.

While the destroyer sped home, I wrote down hurriedly the impressions of the surrender ceremony which Shigemitsu took to the Throne immediately after our return to the Capital, as the Emperor was anxiously waiting for his report. At the end of this report, in which I dwelt at length upon the superb address of the Supreme Commander, I raised a question whether it would have been possible for us, had we been victorious, to embrace the vanquished with a similar magnanimity. Clearly it would have been different. Returning from the audience, Shigemitsu told me that the Emperor nodded with a sigh in agreement. Indeed, a distance inexpressible by numbers separates us—America from Japan. After all, we were not beaten on the battlefield by dint of superior arms. We were defeated in the spiritual contest by virtue of a nobler idea. The real issue was moral—beyond all the powers of algebra to compute.

The day will come when recorded time, age on age, will seem but a point in retrospect. However, happen what may in the future, this Big Day on the *Missouri* will stand out as one of the brightest dates in history, with General MacArthur as a shining obelisk in the desert of human endeavor that marks a timeless march onward toward an enduring peace."

This most favorable impression of a Japanese diplomat differed completely with everything that the Japanese government had been telling its people for years. The philosophy I had expressed, based upon the truth that men may be destroyed by what they have and what they know, but that they may be saved by what they are, produced a most favorable result, immediate and unqualified. Just as I understood them, so they reacted with irresistible energy in the creation of a new Japan.

Trying to recall my emotions and impressions as I prepared to receive the surrender of the mighty warlords of the Far East, I wish that my

pen were wielded by one on such intimate terms with words—those immortal heralds of thought which at the touch of genius become radiant— that at my call they would convey my feelings in terms that would satisfy the ultimate sources of reason, history, and interpretation. For I have a consciousness that in the events culminating at this immortal moment lie those truths which at last are transplanted into epics and lyrics, and those exalted terms which we find on the lips of the great seers and prophets.

Was the day beclouded by mists and trailing clouds? Were there lone trees cresting Tokyo's shores against the moving sky? Were there voices of waters falling far up within some wild ravine racing into the bay? Were there nearby fields where bees were buzzing? I cannot remember, but this I do—the all-embracing pride I felt in my country's monumental victory. Its future seemed to gleam as though seen through the optimistic gates of youth.

I told myself, the tide of world affairs may ebb and flow, old empires may die, new nations be born; alliances may arise, thrive, wither and vanish—but in its effort to build economic growth and prosperity, an atmosphere of hope and freedom, a community of strength and unity of purpose, a lasting peace of justice, my own beloved country now leads the world. It points the way to an age of evolution, in which the brain of man will abstract from the universe its fundamental secrets. Today's wonders will become tomorrow's obsolescence. We stand on the threshold of a new life. What vast panoramas will open before us none can say. They are there, just beyond the horizon, just over there. And they are of a magnificence and a diversity far beyond the comprehension of anyone here today. This new world would have no boundaries—no lost horizons. Its limits would be as broad as the spirit and the imagination of man.

But with this exaltation of pride, my soul saddened as my thoughts turned to my faithful men-at-arms. I had seen them die at Verdun, at St. Mihiel, at Guadalcanal; in the foxholes of Bataan and the batteries of Corregidor; on land, on sea, and in the air; amidst swamp and jungle, hot sands, and frozen reaches; in the knee-deep mud of shell-shocked roads and dripping trenches. They were the driving soul of Americanism. They had given me an abiding faith in the future of this nation—a faith based on the invincible character of the American people. A faith that once again they had restored to our beloved country

Facing page, top:
First meeting of
the Allied Council for Japan.

Facing page, bottom:
The occupation of Japan.

the serenity of hope without fear. A faith in the course of our destiny as a free, prosperous, and happy people.

On September 8, 1945,

I visited Tokyo for the first time. It was just 22 miles from the New Grand Hotel in Yokohama to the American Embassy, which was to be my home throughout the occupation, but they were 22 miles of devastation and vast piles of charred rubble.

I established headquarters in the Dai Ichi Building in downtown Tokyo, across from the moat surrounding the Emperor's palace. The pattern of government was unique in modern annals. I, a professional soldier, had the civil responsibility and absolute control over almost 80-million people, and I would maintain that control until Japan had once more demonstrated that it was ready, willing, and able to become a responsible member of the family of free nations. Never in history had a nation and its people been more completely crushed than were the Japanese at the end of the war. They had suffered more than a military debacle, more than the destruction of their armed forces, more than the elimination of their industrial bases, more even than the occupation of their land by foreign bayonets. Their entire faith in the Japanese way of life, cherished as invincible for many centuries, perished in the agony of their total defeat. The impact of such a disaster was probably greater than had ever been experienced in modern history. The extraordinary feudalism which had prevailed in this isolated land had resulted in almost mythological and fanatical belief in the invincibility of its arms and the superiority of its culture.

Although lacking in iron, coal, metals, cotton, oil, and nearly all commodity essentials, Japan had prospered in the past century largely because of the thrift and industry of its people. By trade and barter it imported raw materials—the wool of Australia, the cotton of America, the rubber and tin and oil of Malaya and the East Indies—and with its cheap labor and transportation supplied the markets of the millions of the coolie class throughout Asia who could not afford the more costly manufactured goods of Europe and America.

Its basic policy and purpose over the years had been to secure the bases which supplied its manufacturing plants. It had absorbed Formosa, Korea, and Manchuria, and was attempting to bring

Reunion in Tokyo
with General Eisenhower.
This was the first meeting
of the two Allied leaders
since 1939.

China under its control. It had prospered and poured billions of its profits into these outlying areas. Indeed, one of the contributing causes of the war had been its fear of the economic sanctions of the Allies initiated by President Roosevelt. Rightly or wrongly, it felt that this course would paralyze its industry and lead to internal revolution. It had hoped to seize and hold the bases contributing to its industrial empire and thus insure for all time its so-called "Greater East Asia Co-Prosperity Sphere."

All during the war its people had been deluded into believing they were winning. Now, in one dreadful moment, all this was to change. Ruin and disaster never conceived possible had engulfed them. In their hour of agony, like all human beings, they turned to their religious faiths to bolster them. But even these failed them at the crucial moment. Shintoism and Buddhism had become so absorbed by governmental control as to be almost an integral part of the fascist hierarchy of leadership.

Because I had been given so much power, I was faced with the most difficult situation of my life. Power is one thing. The problem of how to administer it is another. My professional military knowledge was no longer a major factor. I had to be an economist, a political scientist, an engineer, a manufacturing executive, a teacher, even a theologian of sorts. I had to rebuild a nation that had been almost completely destroyed by the war. Whatever my ethical teachings had been, whatever my basic character was, whatever the concept of mankind that lay within my soul, I would have to bring into this political, economic, and spiritual vacuum concepts of honor, justice, and compassion. Japan had become the world's great laboratory for an experiment in the liberation of a people from totalitarian military rule and for the liberalization of government from within. It was clear that the experiment in Japan must go far beyond the primary purpose of the Allies—the destruction of Japan's ability to wage another war and the punishment of war criminals. Yet history clearly showed that no modern military occupation of a conquered nation had been a success.

Military occupation was not new to me. I had garrisoned the west bank of the Rhine as commander of the Rainbow Division at the end of World War I. At first hand, I had seen what I thought were basic and fundamental weaknesses in prior forms of military occupations: the substitution of civil by military authority; the loss of

self-respect and self-confidence by the people; the constantly growing ascendency of centralized dictatorial power instead of a localized and representative system; the lowering of the spiritual and moral tone of a population controlled by foreign bayonets; the inevitable deterioration in the occupying forces themselves as the disease of power infiltrated their ranks and bred a sort of race superiority. If any occupation lasts too long, or is not carefully watched from the start, one party becomes slaves and the other masters. History teaches, too, that almost every military occupation breeds new wars of the future. I had studied the lives of Alexander and Caesar and Napoleon, and great as these captains were, all had erred when they became the leaders of occupation forces. I tried to remember the lessons my own father had taught me, lessons learned out of his experiences as military governor of the Philippines, but I was assailed by the gravest misgivings. With such hazards as I anticipated, could I succeed? My doubts were to be my best safeguard, my fears my greatest strength.

From the moment of my appointment as supreme commander, I had formulated the policies I intended to follow, implementing them through the Emperor and the machinery of the imperial government. I was thoroughly familiar with Japanese administration, its weaknesses and its strengths, and felt the reforms I contemplated were those which would bring Japan abreast of modern progressive thought and action. First destroy the military power. Punish war criminals. Build the structure of representative government. Modernize the constitution. Hold free elections. Enfranchise the women. Release the political prisoners. Liberate the farmers. Establish a free labor movement. Encourage a free economy. Abolish police oppression. Develop a free and responsible press. Liberalize education. Decentralize the political power. Separate church from state.

These tasks were to occupy me for the next five years and more. All were eventually accomplished, some easily, some with difficulty. But as the reforms progressed and freedom increasingly came to the Japanese masses, a unique bond of mutual faith developed between the Japanese people and the supreme commander. As they increasingly sensed my insistence upon just treatment for them, even at times against the great nations I represented, they came to regard me not as a conqueror, but as a protector. I had a deep responsibility as guardian of these people so dra-

Above:
The Emperor signing
the new Japanese constitution.

Facing page:
General Marshall
visiting Japan.

Philippine Independence Day
ceremonies, Manila,
July 4, 1946.

matically brought under my charge. I felt they needed spiritual leadership as well as material administration. I cautioned our troops from the start that by their conduct our own country would be judged in world opinion, that success or failure of the occupation could well rest upon their poise and self-restraint. Their general conduct was beyond criticism. Many ancient customs of the Japanese, bred by isolation, gave way before the example they set, and admiration for them was aroused in Japanese hearts. They were truly ambassadors of good will.

I carefully abstained from any interferences by edict with the cultural traditions or the personal Japanese way of life. In frequent public statements I advised the Japanese people to seek a healthy blend between the best of theirs and the best of ours, and I was careful to tell them that no people or country was sufficient unto itself in these matters. I encouraged delegations of Japanese from every walk of life to travel in the West, and where it was possible, I paved the way for such visits. I have always felt that one of the things that made the occupation a success was my insistence that we wanted to learn from the Japanese as well as teach them. It had a great deal to do with restoring a sense of dignity and purpose in their people, and as they regained self-respect and pride, they approached an exchange of ideas with avidity and good will. This mutual respect became the foundation of the basic esteem our two peoples came to have for one another— and enabled the occupation to write a unique and warmly human chapter of world history.

While events in Japan continued to progress favorably, many happenings were occurring in other parts of the world.

In Korea, the XXIV Corps, under General Hodge's able leadership had moved in during the aftermath of the war and had occupied the country up to the 38th Parallel, to which line the Russian troops had advanced by the time of Japan's capitulation. South Korea had suffered little damage from the war and led by that fine old patriot, Syngman Rhee, had reorganized and prepared for independence. On August 15, 1948, the Republic of Korea was proclaimed, with Rhee its president. I attended the inaugural ceremonies and was warmly received.

Our troops were withdrawn from Korea, leaving only a military mission to assist in the training of Korean military forces, and Korea was removed from my command, the State Department exercising full control of United States interests, including operational command of the military mission.

In China, Generalissimo Chiang Kai-shek was gradually pushing the Communists back, being largely aided and supplied by the United States. For some unaccountable reason, the Communists were not looked upon with disfavor by the State Department, who labeled them "agrarian reformers." Instead of pushing on to the victory that was within the Generalissimo's grasp, an armistice was arranged, and General Marshall was sent to amalgamate the two opponents. He went by way of Tokyo and stayed with me at the embassy.

After months of fruitless negotiation, he withdrew without tangible results, and the war for China resumed. But in this interval of seven months a decisive change had taken place. The Generalissimo had received no munitions or supplies from the United States, but the Soviets, working day and night, reinforced the Chinese Communist armies. The great mass of military supplies we had sent them at Vladivostok during the latter stages of the war, none of which had been used, was largely transferred to the Chinese forces, so that when hostilities were resumed, the balance of power had shifted. They pressed their advantage to the fullest, and finally drove the Generalissimo's forces out of continental Asia onto Formosa. The decision to withhold previously pledged American support was one of the greatest mistakes ever made in our history. At one fell blow, everything that had been so laboriously built up since the days of John Hay was lost. It was the beginning of the crumbling of our power in continental Asia—the birth of the taunt, "Paper Tiger." Its consequences will be felt for centuries, and its ultimate disastrous effects on the fortunes of the free world are still to be unfolded.

The panorama of events which contributed so decisively to the downfall of our wartime ally, the Republic of China, has never been told to the American people. After the surrender of Japan, events and actions transpired that now seem almost incredible, brought about by ignorance, misinterpretation, and errors of judgment. One of the most accurate comments on this period was made on January 30, 1949, by a young veteran of the war in the Pacific, Congressman John Fitzgerald Kennedy, in an address at Salem, Massachusetts. He said:

Our relationship with China since the end of the Second World War has been a tragic one, and it is of the utmost importance that we search out and spotlight those who must bear the responsibility for our present predicament.

It was clearly enunciated on November 26, 1941, that the independence of China and the stability of the National Government was the fundamental object of our Far Eastern policy. That this and other statements of our policies in the Far East led directly to the attack on Pearl Harbor is well known.

During the postwar period began the great split in the minds of our diplomats over whether to support the Government of Chiang Kai-shek or force Chiang Kai-shek as the price of our assistance to bring Chinese Communists into his government to form a coalition.

Our policy in China has reaped the whirlwind. The continued insistence that aid would not be forthcoming unless a coalition government was formed was a crippling blow to the National Government. So concerned were our diplomats and their advisors . . . with the imperfections of the diplomatic system in China after twenty years of war, and the tales of corruption in higher places, that they lost sight of our tremendous stake in a non-Communist China.

This is the tragic story of China whose freedom we once fought to preserve. What our young men had saved, our diplomats and our President have frittered away.

The failure of those in authority to implement existing United States policy brought about the downfall of an ally and jeopardized the very security of our nation. We have seen the growth of a Communist enemy where we once had a staunch ally. We have watched Communist imperialism spread its influence throughout the world. We have seen thousands of our young men vainly sacrifice their lives in blind pursuit of sterile policies of appeasement based on ignorance of history and of this enemy.

With the formation of the Republic of Korea and the withdrawal of American forces, my official connection with Korea ceased. From August 15, 1948, the doomed little country was under the sole charge of the State Department. But my intelligence section was increasingly aware of the distinct menace of an attack by the North Korean Communists in the summer of 1950.

The Joint Chiefs of Staff reiterated the Administration's unwillingness to commit itself to the defense of South Korea and had recently drawn up a plan of strategic defense in Asia which was based on the assumption that under no circumstances would the United States engage in the military defense of the Korean peninsula.

Above:
Leaving headquarters
in the Dai-Ichi Building.

Below left:
MacArthur and Syngman Rhee. 1948.
Below right: With W. Averell Harriman.

Above left:
General MacArthur as
Supreme Commander
and Director of United Nations
military operations.

Above right:
Mrs. MacArthur officially opening
the "Silk Fair" in Tokyo.
Below:
With Herbert Hoover.

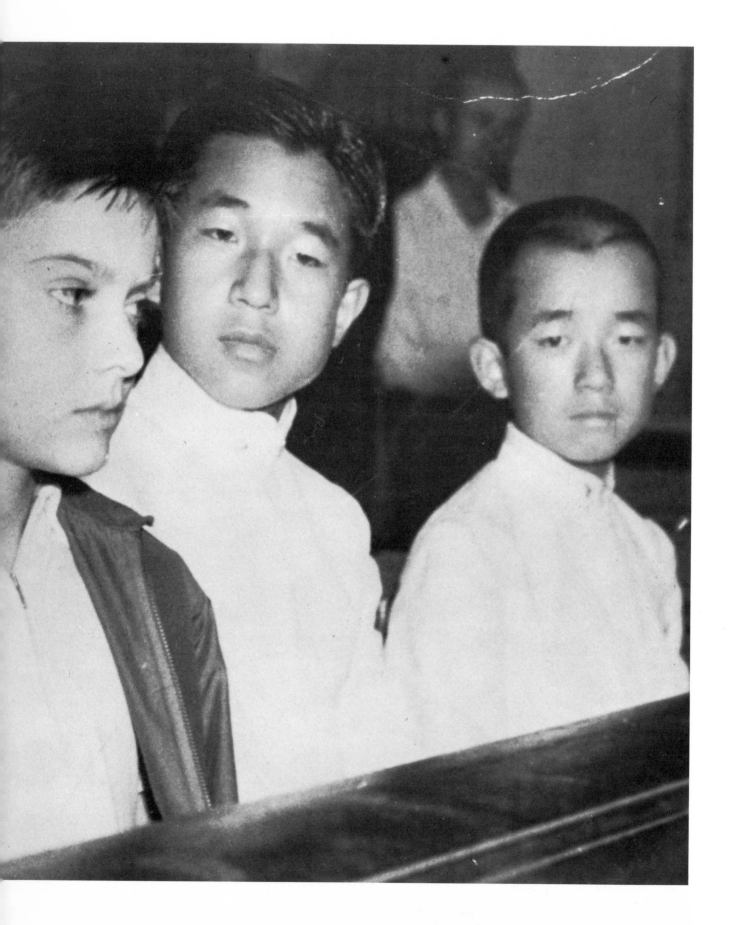

In vain were my attempts to expose the growing Communist threat in the Far East. From June 1949 to June 1950, constant intelligence reports of increasing urgency were submitted to Washington, advising of a possible North Korean thrust. But little impression was made against the general apathy and the inspired "agrarian reform" propaganda. One of these reports even suggested that June 1950 would be the likely time for North Korea to cross the 38th Parallel.

On June 19th, John Foster Dulles, as the personal representative of Secretary Acheson, visited Korea. He had come to Tokyo to discuss a Japanese peace treaty with me, the framework of which I had submitted to Washington. In Korea, he apparently reversed the previous policy enunciated by the State Department, by stating his belief before the Korean legislature that the United States would defend Korea if she were attacked. It made me wonder just what was United States policy in Asia.

Dulles took a brief motor trip from Seoul to the demarcation line between North and South Korea, and what he saw alarmed him not at all. He noted that the South Korean forces appeared quite ready if any attack should come from north of the border. With his tactical inexperience and possible lack of accurate information, Dulles clearly did not realize the inferiority in both troop strength and matériel of the forces he had seen in comparison with their Communist kinsmen above the 38th Parallel.

Left:
With John Foster Dulles.

Facing page:
Arthur MacArthur attending swimming meet with Crown Prince Akahito (center) and Prince Masahito.

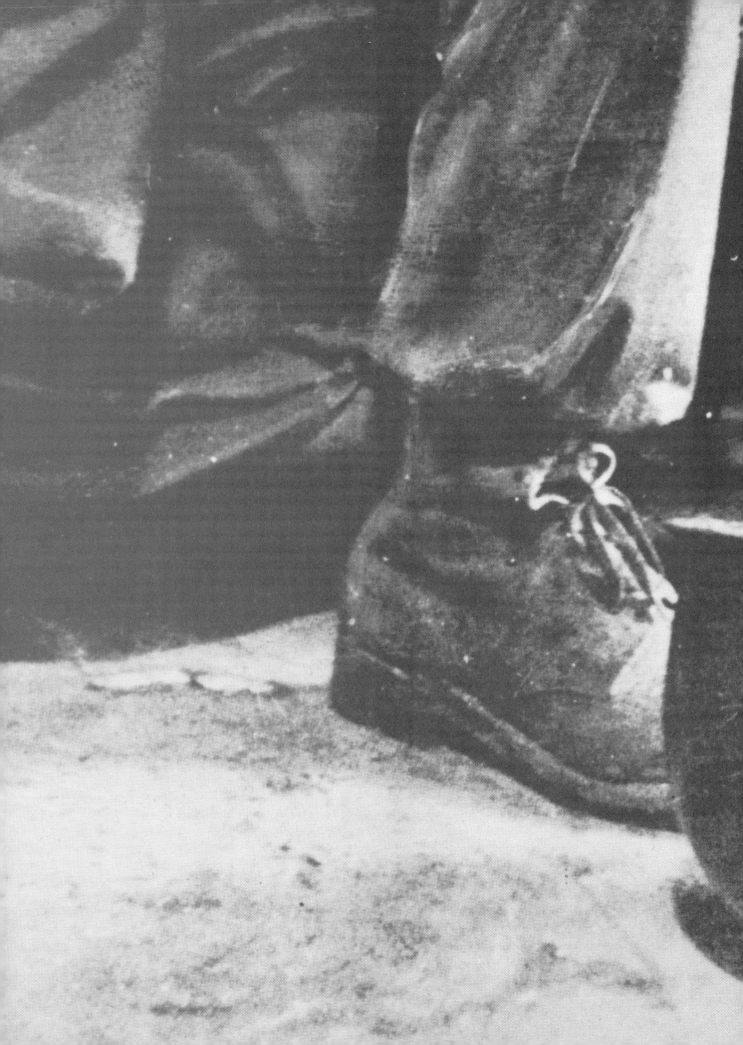

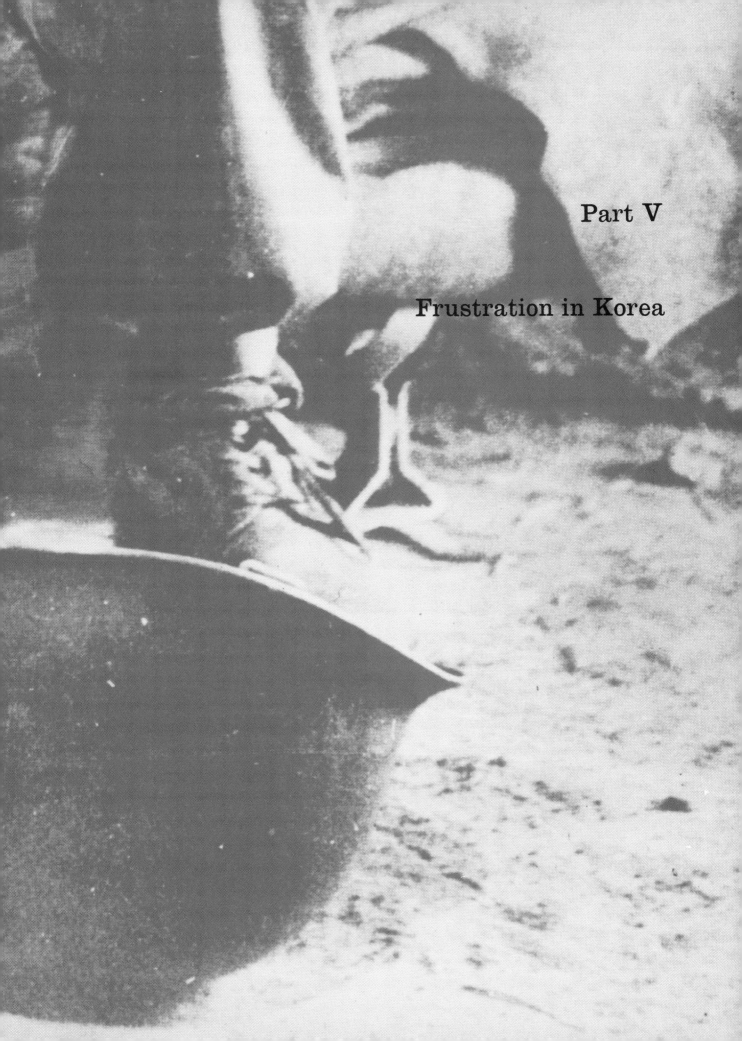

Part V

Frustration in Korea

Sunday, June 25, 1950,

the telephone rang in my bedroom at the American Embassy in Tokyo. It rang with the note of urgency that can sound only in the hush of a darkened room. It was the duty officer at headquarters. "General," he said, "we have just received a dispatch from Seoul, advising that the North Koreans have struck in great strength south across the 38th Parallel at four o'clock this morning." Thousands of Red Korean troops had poured over the border, overwhelming the South Korean advance posts, and were moving southward with a speed and power that was sweeping aside all opposition.

I had an uncanny feeling of nightmare. It had been nine years before, on a Sunday morning, at the same hour, that a telephone call with the same note of urgency had awakened me in the penthouse atop the Manila Hotel. It was the same fell note of the war cry that was again ringing in my ears. It couldn't be, I told myself. Not again! I must still be asleep and dreaming. Not again! But then came the crisp, cool voice of my fine chief of staff, General Ned Almond, "Any orders, General?"

How, I asked myself, could the United States have allowed such a deplorable situation to develop? I thought back to those days, only a short time before, when our country had been militarily more powerful than any nation on earth. General Marshall, then Army chief of staff, had reported to the Secretary of War in 1945: "Never was the strength of American democracy so evident nor has it ever been so clearly within our power to give definite guidance for our course into the future of the human race." But in the short space of five years this power had been frittered away in a bankruptcy of positive and courageous leadership toward any long-range objectives. Again I asked myself, "What is United States policy in Asia?" And the appalling thought came, "The United States has no definite policy in Asia."

Dulles had returned to Tokyo and wired the

Secretary of State Dean Acheson:

Believe that if it appears the South Koreans cannot themselves contain or repulse the attack, United States forces should be used even though this risks Russian counter moves. To sit by while Korea is overrun by unprovoked armed attack would start a world war.

The only immediate military obligation involving my own forces had to do with the evacuation of 2,000 American and United Nations personnel from the area of the Korean Republic. Late on Sunday, the American Ambassador to Korea, John Muccio, asked that they be brought out. I acted immediately. Within minutes, flights of transport planes were rising off runways in Japan and ships at sea were swinging about and heading full draft toward Korean ports. When enemy aircraft began to threaten, I sent in our warplanes from Japan. The operation was successfully concluded without the loss of a single man, woman, or child.

Geographically, South Korea is a ruggedly mountainous peninsula that juts out toward Japan from the Manchurian mainland between the Yellow Sea and the Sea of Japan. An uneven north-south corridor cuts through the rough heart of the country below the 38th Parallel, and there are highways and rail links on both the eastern and western coastal plains.

The South Koreans had four divisions along the 38th Parallel. They had been well trained, and the personnel were brave and patriotic, but they were equipped and organized as a constabulary force, not as troops of the line. They had only light weapons, no air or naval forces, and were lacking in tanks, artillery, and many other essentials. The decision to equip and organize them in this way had been made by the State Department. The argument advanced by the State Department for its decision was that it was a necessary measure to prevent the South Koreans from attacking North Korea, a curiously myopic reasoning that, of course, opened the way for a North Korean attack. It was a vital and a fatal error not to prepare South Korea to meet an attack from the north. The potential of such an attack was inherent in the fact that the North Korean forces had tanks, heavy artillery, and fighter aircraft with which South Korea was not equipped.

The decision was made in Washington by men who understood little about the Pacific and practically nothing about Korea. While they idealistically attempted to prevent the South Koreans from unifying the country by force, they inevitably

Above:
Korea. "We have just received a dispatch from Seoul advising that the North Koreans have struck in great strength south across the 38th parallel at four this morning."

Right:
During a visit to Sunon.

encouraged the North Koreans along opposite lines. Such a fundamental error is inescapable when the diplomat attempts to exercise military judgment, and the result in Korea was that 100,000 United States-trained constabulary troops, with few weapons besides their rifles, were opposed by a Soviet-trained North Korean army of 200,000 men equipped with every modern adjunct of war.

The Communists showed great shrewdness in masking their preparations for attack. Along the 38th Parallel itself they deployed only a lightly armored force similar to that of their neighbors to the south. But this was only a screen for the purpose of deception. Back of this first line of offense, they concentrated a powerful striking army, fully equipped with heavy weapons, including the latest model of Soviet tanks. The thrust across the border was launched by the lightly armed first line which then swung right and left, while the heavy main force charged through the gap, moving irresistibly southward, sweeping the lightly armed South Korean defenders before it.

Even then, it was evident that this was far more than a "police action," as President Truman was to euphemistically characterize it, far more than any localized clean-up of border-raiding North Koreans. In Korea, Communism had hurled its first challenge to war against the free world. Now was the time for decision. Now it was as clear as it would ever be that this was a battle against imperialistic Communism. Now was the time to recognize what the history of the world has taught from the beginning of time: that timidity breeds conflict, and courage often prevents it.

Momentous decisions were being made in Washington and Lake Success that Sunday afternoon. At the request of the United States, United Nations Secretary-General Trygve Lie called the Security Council delegates into a special session. The Russians, who were boycotting the United Nations in protest against membership of the Chinese Nationalists, did not have a delegate present. The United States proposed a resolution condemning the action of the North Korean forces as a breach of the peace, and (1) called for the immediate cessation of hostilities and for the authorities of North Korea to withdraw forthwith their armed forces to the 38th Parallel; (2) requested that the United Nations Temporary Commission on Korea communicate its fully considered recommendations on the situation at once, observe the withdrawal of the North Korean forces to the 38th

Parallel, and advise the Security Council upon compliance with its resolution; and (3) called upon all members to render every assistance to the United Nations in the execution of the resolution and to refrain from giving assistance to the North Korean authorities.

President Truman immediately interpreted the United Nations call to "render every assistance" as an authorization to assist the South Koreans militarily. No one in Washington was quite ready to commit the United States completely, so by "telecom" I was directed to use the Navy and the Air Force to assist South Korean defenses by whatever use I could make of these two arms. I was ordered also to isolate the Nationalist-held island of Formosa from the Chinese mainland. The United States Seventh Fleet was turned over to my operational control for this purpose, and I was specifically directed to prevent any Nationalist attacks on the mainland, as well as to defend the island against Communist attacks.

On June 27th, the United Nations Security Council met again and passed another resolution. In this one, after noting the events, and particularly the failure of the North Korean authorities to desist from the attack and withdraw their military forces to the 38th Parallel, the Security Council concluded that "urgent military measures are required to restore international peace and security," and recommended "that the members of the United Nations furnish such assistance to the Republic of Korea as may be necessary to repel the armed attack."

Thus, step by hesitant step, the United States went to war against Communism in Asia. I could not help being amazed at the manner in which this great decision was being made. With no submission to Congress, whose duty it is to declare war, and without even consulting the field commander involved, the members of the executive branch of the government agreed to enter the Korean War. All the risks inherent in this decision—including the possibility of Chinese and Russian involvement—applied then just as much as they applied later.

My immediate problems were pressing ones. Would United States air and naval forces be enough? Could the South Korean defenders, supported by these forces and supplied with armor, make a successful stand against the powerful war machine that was rolling down upon them from the north? Or would United States ground troops have to be thrown into the battle after all South

Korea was lost? In past wars there was only one way for me to learn such things. There was only one way now. I decided to go to Korea and see for myself.

The morning of June 29th was rainy and overcast as I climbed into the *Bataan.* The news from Korea seemed even more disastrous than it had the day before. The capital city of Seoul was under heavy attack, and the South Korean government had moved to temporary headquarters at Taejon.

The gloom of the day and the even gloomier news dispatches were lightened when I received a message relayed to the plane that the British Asiatic Fleet had been placed under my command. I had long been associated with British fighting units and had the greatest admiration for them. Their professional excellence, their splendid martial bearing, and their unfailing courtesy had long since endeared them to me. I knew that come what may I could count on them to see me through.

The *Bataan* landed at Suwon, 20 miles south of Seoul, through clouds of oily smoke from some bombed and strafed transports which had just been attacked and destroyed. I commandeered a jeep and headed north toward the Han River under constant air bombardment, through the dreadful backwash of a defeated and dispersed army. The South Korean forces were in complete and disorganized flight. We reached the banks of the Han just in time to be caught up in the last rearguard action to defend its bridges.

Seoul was already in enemy hands. Only a mile away, I could see the towers of smoke rising from the ruins of this fourteenth-century city. I pushed forward toward a hill a little way ahead. It was a tragic scene. Across the Han, Seoul burned and smoked in its agony of destruction. There was the constant crump of Red mortar fire as the enemy swooped down toward the bridges. Below me, and streaming by both sides of the hill, were the retreating, panting columns of disorganized troops, the drab color of their weaving lines interspersed here and there with the bright red crosses of ambulances filled with broken, groaning men. The sky was resonant with shrieking missiles of death, and everywhere were the stench and utter desolation of a stricken battlefield. Clogging all the roads in a writhing, dust-shrouded mass of humanity were the refugees. But among them there was no hysteria, no whimpering. Here were the progeny of a proud and sturdy race that for centuries had accepted disaster imperturbably. As they painfully plodded south, carrying all their

General J. Lawton Collins,
Chief of Staff, U.S.A.,
presents the United Nations flag
to General MacArthur.

worldly belongings on their backs, and leading their terror-stricken but wide-eyed, uncrying children, I watched for an hour the pitiful evidence of the disaster I had inherited. In that brief interval on the blood-soaked hill, I formulated my plans. They were desperate plans indeed, but I could see no other way except to accept a defeat which would include not only Korea, but all of continental Asia.

The scene along the Han was enough to convince me that the defensive potential of South Korea had already been exhausted. There was nothing to stop the Communists from rushing their tank columns straight down the few good roads from Seoul to Pusan at the end of the peninsula. All Korea would then be theirs. Even with air and naval support, the South Koreans could not stop the enemy's headlong rush south. Only the immediate commitment of ground troops could possibly do so. The answer I had come to seek was there. I would throw my occupation soldiers into this breach. Completely outnumbered, I would rely upon strategic maneuver to overcome the great odds against me. It would be desperate, but it was my only chance.

And what of Japan? Japan was where my primary responsibility lay. Only a few hours before, my most recent directive from Washington had reiterated that no action I took to protect South Korea should prejudice the protection of Japan. Could I denude this great bastion of troops without inviting Soviet entry from the north? Could I improvise native forces in Japan sufficient to deter any abortive seizure of that country by an enemy if I took elements of the pitifully thin American forces there and committed them in Korea? Could I salvage the time necessary to bring my forces to Pusan? Could I find the transportation to carry the troops to Korea, the munitions and supplies to sustain them in combat, the minimum equipment to create and organize a Japanese protective force? Could I rally, reorganize, and reinspire the defeated Korean army? Could I, if all this were accomplished and the enemy's tenuous supply lines extended to dangerous limits, cut these lines, then envelop and destroy his main forces with only a handful of troops available? I would be outnumbered almost three to one. But in these reflections the genesis of the Inchon operation began to take shape—a counter-stroke that could in itself wrest victory from defeat. I immediately wired Washington:

The South Korean forces are in confusion. Organized and equipped as a light force for maintenance of interior order, they were unprepared for attack by armor and air. Conversely they are incapable of gaining the initiative over such a force as that embodied in the North Korean Army. The South Koreans had made no preparation for defense in depth, for echelons of supply or for a supply system. No plans had been made, or if made were not executed, for the destruction of supplies or materials in the event of a retrograde movement. As a result they have either lost or abandoned their supplies and heavier equipment and have absolutely no system of intercommunication. In most cases the individual soldier in his flight to the south has retained his rifle or carbine. They are gradually being gathered up by an advanced group of my officers I sent over for the purpose. Without artillery, mortars and anti-tank guns, they can only hope to retard the enemy through the fullest utilization of natural obstacles and under the guidance of leadership of high quality. The civilian populace is tranquil, orderly and prosperous according to their scale of living. They have retained a high degree of national spirit and firm belief in the Americans. The roads leading south from Seoul are crowded with refugees refusing to accept the Communist rule.

It is essential that the enemy advance be held or its impetus will threaten the over-running of all of Korea. The South Korean Army is incapable of counteraction and there is a grave danger of a further breakthrough. If the enemy advances continue much further, it will threaten the Republic.

The only assurance for holding the present line and the ability to regain later the lost ground is through the introduction of United States ground combat forces into the Korean battle area. To continue to utilize the forces of our air and navy without an effective ground element can not be decisive. Unless provision is made for the full utilization of the Army-Navy-Air team in this shattered area, our mission will at best be needlessly costly in life, money and prestige. At worst, it might be doomed.

Within twenty-four hours, President Truman authorized the use of ground troops. The number of combat elements which might be withdrawn from Japan without impairing that country's safety was left to my discretion. Thus the United States accepted Communism's challenge to combat in Korea. The risk that the Soviet or the Chinese Communists might enter the war was clearly understood and defiantly accepted. The American tradition had always been that once our troops are committed to battle, the full power and means of the nation would be mobilized and dedicated to fight for victory—not for stalemate or compromise. And I set out to chart the strategic course which

Above:
Generals Collins and
Vandenberg visiting
General MacArthur in Tokyo
to discuss the Korean situation.

Below:
Mrs. MacArthur embraces
her husband upon
his return from Korea.

would make that victory possible. Not by the wildest stretch of imagination did I dream that this tradition might be broken.

In Japan, I had four occupation divisions, the 7th, 24th, 25th, and 1st Cavalry, comprising the Eighth Army, with garrisons extending from Kyushu to Hokkaido. The army commander was General Walton Walker, a seasoned and experienced officer who had been one of George Patton's corps commanders in the European war. The Air Force was under Lieutenant General George E. Stratemeyer, and the Navy under Admiral C. Turner Joy, both able and efficient veterans of the war. All of my old commanders and most of my staff had long since returned to the United States.

The occupation infantry in Japan was one-third below strength. The regiments had only two instead of three battalions, light tanks instead of heavy, 105-mm. howitzers instead of 155-mm. cannon. The Korean War meant entry into action "as is." No time out for recruiting rallies or to build up and get ready. It was move in—and shoot. This put the bulk of the burden on the G.I. The story of the infantry soldier is an old and honorable one. He carries his home with him—and often his grave. Somehow, he has to bring along the whole paraphernalia of fighting, as well as domesticated living: the grocery store, the ration dump; the hospital, the Medical Corps; the garage, the motor pool; the telephone, the Signal Service. He must sleep and eat and fight and die on foot, in all weather, rain or shine, with or without shelter. He is vulnerable day and night. Death has his finger on him for twenty-four hours, in battle, going toward it, or retreating from it. It is a wonder that the morale of those uniformed gypsies never falters.

The North Koreans had advanced across the 38th Parallel in an estimated strength of six infantry divisions and three constabulary brigades, spearheaded by nearly 200 Soviet tanks, with supporting units of heavy artillery, all under cover of an air umbrella. The main attack was along the central corridor, with simultaneous attacks to the west and down the east-coast road, and amphibious landings at various South Korean coastal points. They crossed the Han River, and South Korean resistance became increasingly unsuccessful.

The immediate necessity was to slow down the Red advance before it enveloped all of Korea. My only chance to do this was to commit my forces piecemeal as rapidly as I could get them to the front, relying upon the stratagem that the presence of American ground forces in the battle area would chill the enemy commander into taking precautionary and time-consuming methods. By this method of buying time for space I could build up a force at Pusan, which would serve as a base for future operations. Speed in getting the troops to Korea was of the essence. Every ship, every plane, every train was commandeered. Never had I known such a fast mobilization to a battle front. Elements of the 24th Division were first in by air. Roadblocks were thrown up and defended desperately. Every artifice of harassment and deception was practiced, and the stratagem worked.

The effect of American ground troops, however small in number, resisting the enemy advance confirmed my hopes. The enemy commander at once brought his advance to a stop to permit the laborious bringing up of artillery from across the river without benefit of the regular bridges, which our air force by then had destroyed. He had no way of knowing either the strength of the American forces already committed, and in their immediate support, or what change in the battle situation their presence presaged. He decided, as I had anticipated, against taking any chance. So, instead of continuing to drive his tank columns forward, he deployed all of his forces across the difficult terrain in conventional line of battle. This was his fatal error. It had exacted a painful sacrifice from my men committed to this unequal battle, but it paid off in precious time, so essential if any tactic in the prevailing situation was to be successful.

During those first days of American fighting in South Korea, I threw in troops by air in the hope of establishing a locus of resistance around which I could rally the fast-retreating South Korean forces. I had hoped by that arrogant display of strength to fool the enemy into a belief that I had greater resources at my disposal than I did. We gained ten days by this process before the enemy had deployed in line of battle along the 150-mile front, with Suwon as the pivotal point. By that time, I had brought forth the rest of the 24th Division, under Major General William F. Dean, with orders to delay the enemy until I could bring the 1st Cavalry Division and the 25th Division over from Japan. Dean fought a very desperate series of isolated combats in which a large part of that division was destroyed.

By the time this had happened, the enemy commander had realized his mistake. He had been stopped not by a massive American defensive

투루맨 大統領

美國大統領의 聲明

―大韓民國에 對한 北鮮軍侵略에 關하여―

「國際聯合會 安全保障理事會는 北鮮侵略軍에 對하여
戰鬪를 中止하고 北緯三十八度線以北으로 撤退하라고 勸告하였
습니다. 그러나 이 勸告는 實現되지못하였으며 그 反對로 그 敵對行爲는 强히 繼續되었습
니다. 國際安全保障理事會는 國際聯合會 全加盟國, 代表에게 이 決意를 實行하는
데 對하여 積極的으로 國際聯合會로 援助하라고 要請하였습니다. 이러한 情勢에
따라. 余는 美國極東空軍과 海軍에게 大韓民國政府軍隊를 掩護하고 援助하라고
命令하였습니다. 余는 大韓民國에 對한 이 攻擊은 明白히 共産主義者들이 陰謀工作
으로 獨立國家를 征服할 政策을 放棄하고 지금 부러는 武力의 爲한 直接行動을
取하는것입니다. 口

Leaflet distributed to the people of South Korea, containing a statement
by the President of the United States concerning North Korean aggression.

force, but merely by the appearance of force—by that arrogant display of strength. He moved rapidly to make up for the time he had lost, but it was too late. I had by this time established the Eighth Army in Korea. The enemy, though, still had an enormous superiority in manpower and weight and quality of arms. Aided by this preponderance of numbers and weapons, he was able simultaneously to exert heavy pressure against General Walker's men in the center and flow around them on both sides.

On July 7th, 1950

I made my first call to Washington for reinforcements. In a message to the Joint Chiefs of Staff I explained that we were facing "an aggressive and well trained professional army operating under excellent top level guidance and demonstrated superior command of strategic and tactical principles." My immediate need was for not less than five full-strength divisions and three tank battalions, together with reinforcing artillery and service elements. My ultimate purpose, I said, was "fully to exploit our air and sea control and, by amphibious maneuver, strike behind his mass of ground forces." Should Soviet Russia or Communist China intervene, I added, "a new situation would develop which is not predictable now."

I was amazed when this message of desperate need for the necessary strength to implement a Washington decision was disapproved by Washington itself. The reasons given were that: (1) no increase in any part of the armed services had been authorized; (2) a suitable United States military posture in other parts of the world had to be maintained; and (3) there was a shortage of shipping. What all this amounted to actually was the old faulty principle of "priorities," under which the Far East was again at the bottom of the list. That it reaffirmed a principle that had lost us the Philippines and immeasurably retarded the defeat of Japan was surprising enough in itself, but the circumstances under which the decision was being formulated made it almost unbelievable. The all-important difference, of course, was that while during World War II we had been fighting in Europe, now we were not. And it could not fail to be obvious even to the non-military mind that Soviet military dispositions in eastern Europe were defensive rather than offensive. I repeated my original request. It was again disapproved.

The Security Council of the United Nations on July 7th, directed the establishment of a unified Korean command. The United States was to be the U.N.'s operative agent, and was instructed to appoint the over-all commander. The next day President Truman named me commander-in-chief, and (the Republic of Korea was not a U.N. member) President Syngman Rhee signified his government's approval of the appointment.

On July 8th, I authorized Japan to increase its defense force by approximately 100,000 men, and in Korea brought our units up to full strength by integrating Koreans into the ranks. This was the so-called "buddy system" which proved so successful. While I could obtain only a trickle of soldiers from Washington, under the plea that they were needed in Germany where there was no war, the local governments, just as in the Pacific war, supported my efforts with every fiber of their being.

By July 20th, the period of piecemeal entry into action was over, the painful rearguard type of retreat under pressure of overwhelming numbers was ended, the fight for time against space was won. The enemy's plan and great opportunity depended upon the speed with which he could overrun South Korea once he had breached the Han River line. This chance he had now lost through the extraordinary speed with which the Eighth Army had been deployed from Japan to stem his rush. When he crashed the Han line, the way seemed entirely open and victory was within his grasp. The desperate decision to throw in piecemeal American elements as they arrived by every available means of transport from Japan was the only hope to save the situation. The skill and valor thereafter displayed in successive holding actions by the ground forces in accordance with this concept, brilliantly supported in complete co-ordination by air and naval elements, forced the enemy into continued deployments, mostly frontal attacks, and confused logistics which so slowed his advance and blunted his drive that we bought the precious time necessary to build a secure base. With the issue fully joined, our future action could be predicated on choice. We now held South Korea, and, in the face of overwhelming numbers, had relatively few casualties.

The area in which I had military responsibility having been enlarged to include Formosa and the Pescadore Islands, I felt it necessary, late in July, to visit the island in order to determine its military capabilities for defense.

Among the problems which were discussed was the prompt and generous offer of the Nationalist Chinese to send troops to join the United Nations forces in Korea. The belief of all concerned, however, was that such action at this time might so seriously jeopardize the defense of Formosa that it would be inadvisable. Arrangements were completed for effective co-ordination between the American forces under my command and those of the Chinese Nationalists, the better to meet any attack which a hostile force might be foolish enough to attempt. Such an attack would, in my opinion, stand little chance of success. It was a great pleasure for me to meet my old comrade-in-arms of the last war, Generalissimo Chiang Kai-shek. His indomitable determination to resist Communist domination aroused my sincere admiration.

To my astonishment, the visit to Formosa and my meeting with Chiang Kai-shek was greeted by a furor. My habitual critics, including those within the United Nations who advocated appeasement of the Soviet Union and Red China, naturally set in with their cudgels, but I was somewhat startled to find myself attacked by certain groups within the United States itself. It did not dawn on me that my visit to Formosa would be construed as political or in any way undesirable. I was merely trying to make my own military estimate of the situation. There was such a frenzy of irresponsible diatribe, some of the misrepresentations so gross and obviously malicious, that I felt it necessary to make a further statement:

There have been so many misstatements made with reference to my trip to Formosa that in the public interest at this critical moment I feel constrained to correct them. This trip was formally arranged and coordinated beforehand with all branches of the American and Chinese Governments. It was limited entirely to military matters, as I stated in my public release after the visit, and dealt solely with the problem of preventing military violence to Formosa as directed by the President—the implementation of which directive is my responsibility. It had no connection with political affairs and, therefore, no suggestion or thought was ever made from any source whatsoever that a political representative accompany me. The subject of the future of the Chinese Government, of developments on the Chinese mainland, or anything else outside the scope of my own military responsibility was not discussed or even mentioned. Full reports on the results of the visit were promptly made to Washington. This visit has been maliciously misrepresented to the public by those who invariably in the past have propagandized a policy of defeatism and appeasement in the Pacific. I hope the American people will not be misled by sly insinuations, brash speculations and bold misstatements invariably attributed to anonymous sources, so insidiously fed them both nationally and internationally by persons ten thousand miles away from the actual events, which tend, if they are not indeed designed, to promote disunity and destroy faith and confidence in American institutions and American representatives at this time of great world peril.

The Administration apparently became somewhat alarmed at our deteriorating prestige in the Orient, and President Truman issued a public statement saying: "The occupation of Formosa by Communist forces would be a direct threat to the security of the Pacific area and to the United States forces performing their lawful and necessary functions in that area."

I received the following message from President Truman: "At my direction, my assistant, W. Averell Harriman, will leave here Friday 4 August by air to confer with you in Tokyo on political aspects of Far Eastern situation. Announcement of mission will be made here. Warm regards."

As special envoy from President Truman, Averell Harriman was sent to Tokyo to advise the President on political aspects of the Far Eastern situation. Harriman and I were friends of long standing. While superintendent of West Point I had hunted ducks on his preserve near Tuxedo. We discussed fully global conditions. I found him careful and cautious in what he said, but gained these very definite impressions: that there was no fixed and comprehensive United States policy for the Far East; that foreign influences, especially those of Great Britain, were very powerful in Washington; that there was no apparent interest in mounting an offensive against the Communists; that we were content to attempt to block their moves, but not to initiate any counter-moves; that we would defend Formosa if attacked, just as we had done in Korea; that President Truman had conceived a violent animosity toward Chiang Kai-shek; and that anyone who favored the Generalissimo might well arouse the President's disfavor. He left me with a feeling of concern and uneasiness that the situation in the Far East was little understood and mistakenly downgraded in high circles in Washington.

On August 17th, I received an invitation from the commander-in-chief of the Veterans of Foreign Wars to send a message to be read at their forthcoming annual encampment. I had sent messages to many other organizations in the past and regarded it as a matter of routine. The message expressed my personal opinion of the strategic importance of Formosa and its relation to our defensive position in the Pacific. There was nothing political in it. I sent it throught the Department of the Army ten days before the encampment. The officials of that Department apparently found nothing objectionable in it. It was in complete support of the President's announced policy toward Formosa. It actually contained this paragraph:

The decision of President Truman on June 27th lighted into a flame a lamp of hope throughout Asia that was burning dimly toward extinction. It marked for the Far East the focal and turning point in this area's struggle for freedom. It swept aside in one great monumental stroke all of the hypocrisy and the sophistry which has confused and deluded so many people distant from the actual scene.

A week after sending the message I received a wire in the name of the "President of the United States" directing that I withdraw the message to the Veterans of Foreign Wars. The reason given was that "various features with respect to Formosa are in conflict with the policy of the United States." I was utterly astonished. I sent for a copy of the message and re-examined it, but could find no feature that was not in complete support of the President.

I replied, "My message was most carefully prepared to fully support the President's policy position. My remarks were calculated only to support his declaration and I am unable to see wherein they might be interpreted otherwise. The views were purely my personal ones and the subject had previously been freely discussed in all circles, governmental and private, both at home and abroad." To this day I do not know who managed to construe my statement as meaning exactly the opposite of what it said, and how this person or persons could have so easily deceived the President. Were his political advisers playing strategist, and his military advisers playing politics?

On August 30th, only two days later, I received this letter from the President: "I am sending you for your information the text of a letter which I sent to Ambassador Warren Austin (U.S. Ambassador to the United Nations) addressed to Trygve Lie on August 25. You will understand why my action of the 26th in directing the withdrawal of your message to the Veterans of Foreign Wars was necessary." The letter contained seven points:

1. The United States has not encroached on the territory of China, nor has the United States taken aggressive action against China.

2. The action of the United States in regard to Formosa was taken at a time when that island was the scene of conflict with the mainland. More serious conflict was threatened by the public declaration of the Chinese Communist authorities.

3. The action of the United States was an impartial neutralizing action addressed both to the forces on Formosa and to those on the mainland. We have no designs on Formosa and our action was not inspired by any desire to acquire a special position for the United States.

4. The action of the United States was expressly stated to be without prejudice to the future political settlement of the status of the island. The actual status of the island is that it is territory taken from Japan by the victory of the Allied Forces in the Pacific. Like other such territories, its legal status cannot be fixed until there is international action to determine its future. The Chinese Government was asked by the Allies to take the surrender of the Japanese forces on the island. That is the reason the Chinese are there now.

5. The United States has a record through history of friendship for the Chinese people. We still feel the friendship and know that millions of Chinese reciprocate it.

6. The United States would welcome United Nations consideration of the case of Formosa.

7. Formosa is now at peace and will remain so unless someone resorts to force. If the Security Council wishes to study the question of Formosa we shall support and assist that study.

What was significant about the letter was that its basic premise, as set forth in item 4, was simply not correct. At Cairo on December 1, 1943, an agreement was entered into between the United States, China, and the United Kingdom, represented respectively by President Roosevelt, Generalissimo Chiang, and Prime Minister Churchill. The agreement which they all signed reads in part as follows:

It is their purpose that Japan shall be stripped of all the islands in the Pacific which she had seized or occupied since the beginning of the first World War in 1914, and that the territories Japan has stolen from the Chinese, such as Manchuria, Formosa, and the Pescadores, shall be restored to the Republic of China.

That, and only that, was the reason why Formosa was given to China at the end of World War II. There was no further need to settle the question of who owned Formosa; as far as we were concerned, the Republic of China owned Formosa by the terms of the agreement at Cairo.

My opinion of the strategic importance of Formosa was shared by the Joint Chiefs of Staff. On September 1st, they officially recommended that the island and its disposition be kept out of any political bargaining at a forthcoming meeting of the foreign ministers. "The strategic consequences of a Communist-dominated Formosa," the Joint Chiefs advised, "would be so seriously detrimental to United States security that in the opinion of the Joint Chiefs of Staff, the United States should not permit the disposition of Formosa to be recommended in the first instance or decided by any commission or agency of the United Nations."

But the pressure against our Nationalist Chinese ally of World War II did not cease. It had started immediately after the war's end, with the argument, mentioned before, that the Chinese Communists were really only "agrarian reformers" —a claim that has become one of modern history's bitterest jests. It was, of course, given its greatest impetus when General Marshall made the tragic mistake of using American prestige as a lever for attempting to force a coalition government on Chiang Kai-shek. And it manifested itself most vocally when I tried to implement the President's directive to defend Formosa by strengthening the alliance between Nationalist and United States military forces.

The arguments took many forms. At first, the claim was that Chiang's government was corrupt. Somehow, the reasoning ran, rule by the Kuomintang was even worse than a Communist police state, and, therefore, any change would be for the better. Why they would ally with the same Chiang against the Japanese, but not against the Communists, was never clear. But it was perfectly clear to me now that it was only a question of time when my head would roll.

On August 20th, the atrocities being committed by the North Koreans on prisoners caused me to advise the enemy's commander-in-chief that unless immediate orders were given for the cessation of such brutality, I would hold each and every enemy commander criminally accountable under the rules and precedents of war.

From this time on there was a marked decrease in such atrocities and a noteworthy improvement in the enemy's handling of prisoners.

The month of August in Korea witnessed repeated and savage attacks on our forces. But the South Koreans had now been rallied and reorganized, and five small R.O.K. divisions—the 1st, 3rd, 6th, 8th, and Capital—were with General Walker. A brigade of the 1st United States Marine Division had also joined the Eighth Army. Our forces made a planned withdrawal from Taejon and accepted battle along the Naktong River. At Yongdong, after a bitter four-day struggle, the enemy overwhelmed our position and forced our withdrawal further south to what amounted to an extended beachhead around Pusan.

The North Koreans now had thirteen divisions at the front. They were fighting not on a continuous line of deployment, but in a series of columns of battalion and regimental size, probing roads and mountain trails in a continuous effort to penetrate and outflank our position. For a time, it was touch and go. The Cassandras of the world gloomily speculated on a vast Asiatic Dunkirk.

The pattern and density of the enemy's supply and reinforcement movement showed that heavy tonnage was coming from Chinese Manchuria and Russian Siberia, through Seoul, in spite of our bombing and strafing. It moved habitually by night. The ingenuity and tenacity in repair of bridges and tracks was of the highest order. Fresh divisions and tank brigades from North Korea arrived constantly. Supply, food, and ammunition went forward without a letup, by train, by truck and motor, by oxcart, and cargodoes. But Walker, his back to the sea, with great skill and courage by all commands and ranks, slowed the enemy to a walk, and by the end of the month had established a fairly stable line of defense. The order was "to stand or die."

With a Japanese force of 100,000 men mustered and well on the road toward securing the safety of Japan from sudden seizure by Russia, with Japan proving its utter loyalty by its well-ordered conduct, with my air and naval forces unopposed, I was now finally ready for the last great stroke to bring my plan into fruition. My Han River dream as a possibility had begun to assume the certainties of reality—a turning movement deep into the flank and rear of the enemy that would sever his supply lines and encircle all his forces south of Seoul. I had made similar decisions in past campaigns, but none more fraught with danger, none that promised to be more vitally conclusive if successful.

The target I selected was Inchon, 20 miles west of Seoul and the second largest port in South Korea. The target date, because of the great tides at Inchon, had to be the middle of September. This meant that the staging for the landing at Inchon would have to be accomplished more rapidly than that of any other large amphibious operation in modern warfare. On July 23rd I had cabled Washington:

Operation planned mid-September is amphibious landing of a two division corps in rear of enemy lines for purpose of enveloping and destroying enemy forces in conjunction with attack from south by Eighth Army. I am firmly convinced that early and strong effort behind his front will sever his main lines of communication and enable us to deliver a decisive and crushing blow. The alternative is a frontal attack which can only result in a protracted and expensive campaign.

My plan was opposed by powerful military influences in Washington. The essence of the operation depended upon a great amphibious movement, but the chairman of the Joint Chiefs of Staff, General Omar Bradley, was of the considered opinion that such amphibious operations were obsolete—that there would never be another successful movement of this sort. He had stirred up a storm in calling Navy personnel, which included Marines "Fancy Dans." President Truman also was not in favor of using the Marines as a major military unit of our armed forces. In a letter to Congressman McDonough of California he said: "The Marine Corps is the Navy's police force and as long as I am President that is what it will remain. They have a propaganda machine that is almost equal to Stalin's."

After a silence of three weeks, the Joint Chiefs of Staff wired me that General Joseph Collins, Army Chief of Staff, and Admiral Forrest Sherman, Chief of Naval Operations, were coming to Tokyo to discuss this maneuver with me. It was evident immediately upon their arrival that the actual purpose of their trip was not so much to discuss as to dissuade.

On August 23rd, I called a strategic conference to debate the problem at the Dai Ichi Building in Tokyo. The conferees included General Collins and Admiral Sherman, as well as Marine Chief Lieutenant General Lemuel C. Shephard Jr.;

my air commander, Stratemeyer; my chief of staff, Almond, whom I had already designated commander of the X Corps, which was to make the Inchon landing; my Navy commander, Joy; my fleet commander, Struble; my amphibious expert, Admiral James T. Doyle; and a gathering of other staff officers and aids making up a veritable constellation of silver stars.

As at the Pearl Harbor conference with Roosevelt and Nimitz in 1944, the Navy presented its case first. A naval briefing staff argued that two elements—tide and terrain—made a landing at Inchon extremely hazardous. They referred to Navy hydrographic studies which listed the average rise and fall of the tides at Inchon at 20.7 feet—one of the greatest in the world. On the tentative target date for the invasion, the rise and fall would be more than 30 feet because of the position of the moon. When Inchon's tides were at full ebb, the mud banks that had accumulated over the centuries from the Yellow Sea jutted from the shore in some places as far as 2 miles out into the harbor. And during ebb and flow these tides raced through "Flying Fish Channel," the best approach to the port, at speeds up to 6 knots. Even under the most favorable conditions "Flying Fish Channel" was narrow and winding. Not only did it make a perfect location for enemy mines, but any ship sunk at a particularly vulnerable point could block the channel to all other ships.

On the target date, the Navy experts went on, the first high tide would occur at 6:59 in the morning, and the afternoon high tide would be at 7:19, a full thirty-five minutes after sunset. Within two hours after high tide most of the assault craft would be wallowing in the ooze of Inchon's mud banks, sitting ducks for Communist shore batteries until the next tide came in to float them again. In effect, the amphibious forces would have only about two hours in the morning for the complex job of reducing or effectively neutralizing Wolmi-do, the 350-foot-high, heavily fortified island which commands the harbor and which is connected with the mainland by a long causeway.

Assuming that this could be done, the afternoon's high tide and approaching darkness would allow only two and a half hours for the troops to land, secure a beachhead for the night, and bring up all the supplies essential to enable forces to withstand counterattacks until morning. The landing craft, after putting the first assault waves ashore, would be helpless on the mud banks until the morning tide.

Beyond all this, the Navy summed up, the assault landings would have to be made right in the heart of the city itself, where every structure provided a potential strong point of enemy resistance. Reviewing the Navy's presentation, Admiral Sherman concluded by saying: "If every possible geographical and naval handicap were listed—Inchon has 'em all."

General Collins then presented his arguments. The Army, its Chief of Staff said, felt that Inchon was too far in the rear of the present battle area to have the necessary immediate effect on the enemy. To accomplish this big maneuver successfully with the limited resources available would require withdrawing the 1st Marine Brigade, which was then holding a sector in Walker's hard pressed defense line, and would thus further endanger that position. Collins was not at all sure, in fact did not believe, that even if I captured Seoul I could make contact with Walker to the south. And furthermore, he said, I might well run into overwhelming enemy force in the area of the capital city and suffer complete defeat.

Collins had an alternate proposal to abandon the plan of the Inchon landing and instead aim for the west-coast port of Kunsan. This port was much further south and presented few of Inchon's physical obstacles. At this point Sherman spoke up and seconded Collins in urging me to give up Inchon in favor of Kunsan.

Sherman and Collins finished their argument. I waited a moment or so to collect my thoughts. I could feel the tension rising in the room. Almond shifted uneasily in his chair. If ever a silence was pregnant, this one was. I could almost hear my father's voice telling me as he had so many years ago, "Doug, councils of war breed timidity and defeatism."

The bulk of the Reds [I said] are committed around Walker's defense perimeter. The enemy, I am convinced, has failed to prepare Inchon properly for defense. The very arguments you have made as to the impracticabilities involved will tend to ensure for me the element of surprise. For the enemy commander will reason that no one would be so brash as to make such an attempt. Surprise is the most vital element for success in war. As an example, the Marquis de Montcalm believed in 1759 that it was impossible for an armed force to scale the precipitous river banks south of the then walled city of Quebec, and therefore concentrated his formidable defenses along the more vul-

Above:
With Vice-Admiral A. D. Struble in Inchon Harbor.

Below:
After landing at Inchon.

Above: Men of the 1st Marine Division.
Below left: North Korean boys
serving in the North Korean
army interrogated by men
of the 2nd Infantry Division.

Below right:
Meeting at Pyong Yang.
Lieutenant Colonel
Anthony Story (left),
MacArthur's pilot.

nerable banks north of the city. But General James Wolfe and a small force did indeed come up the St. Lawrence River and scale those heights. On the Plains of Abraham, Wolfe won a stunning victory that was made possible almost entirely by surprise. Thus he captured Quebec and in effect ended the French and Indian War. Like Montcalm, the North Koreans would regard an Inchon landing as impossible. Like Wolfe, I could take them by surprise.

The Navy's objections as to tides, hydrography, terrain, and physical handicaps are indeed substantial and pertinent. But they are not insuperable. My confidence in the Navy is complete, and in fact I seem to have more confidence in the Navy than the Navy has in itself. The Navy's rich experience in staging the numerous amphibious landings under my command in the Pacific during the late war, frequently under somewhat similar difficulties, leaves me with little doubt on that score.

As to the proposal for a landing at Kunsan, it would indeed eliminate many of the hazards of Inchon, but it would be largely ineffective and indecisive. It would be an attempted envelopment which would not envelop. It would not sever or destroy the enemy's supply lines or distribution center, and would therefore serve little purpose. It would be a "short envelopment," and nothing in war is more futile. Better no flank movement than one such as this. The only result would be a hookup with Walker's troops on his left. It would be better to send the troops directly to Walker than by such an indirect and costly process. In other words, this would simply be sending more troops to help Walker "hang on," and hanging on was not good enough. No decision can be reached by defensive actions in Walker's perimeter. To fight frontally in a breakthrough from Pusan will be bloody and indecisive. The enemy will merely roll back on his lines of supply and communication.

But seizure of Inchon and Seoul will cut the enemy's supply line and seal off the entire southern peninsula. The vulnerability of the enemy is his supply position. Every step southward extends his transport lines and renders them more frail and subject to dislocation. The several major lines of enemy supply from the north converge on Seoul, and from Seoul they radiate to the several sectors of the front. By seizing Seoul I would completely paralyze the enemy's supply system—coming and going. This in turn will paralyze the fighting power of the troops that now face Walker. Without munitions and food they will soon be helpless and disorganized, and can easily be overpowered by our smaller but well-supplied forces.

The only alternative to a stroke such as I propose will be the continuation of the savage sacrifice we are making at Pusan, with no hope of relief in sight. Are you content to let our troops stay in that bloody perimeter like beef cattle in the slaughterhouse? Who will take the responsibility for such a tragedy? Certainly, I will not.

The prestige of the Western world hangs in the balance. Oriental millions are watching the outcome. It is plainly apparent that here in Asia is where the Communist conspirators have elected to make their play for global conquest. The test is not in Berlin or Vienna, in London, Paris or Washington. It is here and now—it is along the Naktong River in South Korea. We have joined the issue on the battlefield. Actually, we here fight Europe's war with arms, while there it is still confined to words. If we lose the war to Communism in Asia, the fate of Europe will be gravely jeopardized. Win it and Europe will probably be saved from war and stay free. Make the wrong decision here—the fatal decision of inertia—and we will be done. I can almost hear the ticking of the second hand of destiny. We must act now or we will die.

If my estimate is inaccurate and should I run into a defense with which I cannot cope, I will be there personally and will immediately withdraw our forces before they are committed to a bloody setback. The only loss then will be my professional reputation. But Inchon will not fail. Inchon will succeed. And it will save 100,000 lives.

I finished. The silence was complete. Then Sherman, an old associate of the Pacific war, rose and said, "Thank you. A great voice in a great cause." And on August 29th I received a wire from the Joint Chiefs of Staff: "We concur after reviewing the information brought back by General Collins and Admiral Sherman, in making preparations and executing a turning movement by amphibious forces on the west coast of Korea—at Inchon."

I planned to use the 7th Division, until this time retained in Japan, and the 1st Marine Division to make the Inchon landing. They were to form the X Corps under Almond. This involved the withdrawal of the 1st Marine Brigade from the perimeter. To compensate to some extent for this withdrawal, a regimental combat team of the 7th Division was to be in floating reserve off Pusan. It could be rushed into any gap that might develop in Walker's line, and, if not, would be the last element to land at Inchon.

No operation of this size could be performed without taking the chance of disclosure. It is to the credit of the many news correspondents at the front who could not fail to witness these troop dispositions and surmise the reason for them, as well as to the credit of their editors back home, that the projected counterattack was a well-kept secret.

By a week before the target date, all the details of the master plan had been worked out. The troops that had come from Japan, the United States, and even the Mediterranean had virtually all arrived. Each unit had been assigned its separate responsibility, and those Marines and soldiers who were not already afloat along Korea's west coast were in the final stages of embarkation. It was at this eleventh hour that I received a message from the Joint Chiefs of Staff which chilled me to the marrow of my bones.

The message expressed doubt of success and implied the whole movement should be abandoned. It read in part: "We have noted with considerable concern the recent trend of events in Korea. In the light of the commitment of all the reserves available to the Eighth Army, we desire your estimate as to the feasibility and chance of success of projected operation if initiated on planned schedule." What could have given rise to such a query at such an hour? Had someone in authority in Washington lost his nerve? Could it be the President? Or Marshall, who had just become Secretary of Defense? Or Bradley? Or was it merely an anticipating alibi if the operation should run into trouble? Whatever lay behind this last-minute hesitancy, it clearly suggested the possibility that even after the millions of man-hours already expended, I might be ordered to abandon it.

I immediately penciled a reply:

I regard the chance of success of the operation as excellent. I go further in belief that it represents the only hope of wresting the initiative from the enemy and thereby presenting the opportunity for a decisive blow. To do otherwise is to commit us to a war of indefinite duration, of gradual attrition and of doubtful result, as the enemy has potentialities of buildup and reinforcements which far exceed our own. Our stroke as planned would prevent any material reinforcements in buildup of the enemy in the present combat zone. The situation within the perimeter is not critical. It is possible that there may be some contraction, and defense positions have been selected for this contingency. There is not the slightest possibility, however, of our forces being ejected from the Pusan beachhead.

The envelopment from the north will instantly relieve the pressure upon the south perimeter and, indeed, is the only way that this can be accomplished. The success of the enveloping movement from the north does not depend upon the rapid juncture of the X Corps with the Eighth Army. The seizure of the beach of the enemy's distributing system in the Seoul area will completely dislocate the logistical supply of his forces now operating in South Korea and therefore will ultimately result in their disintegration. The prompt juncture of our two forces, while it would be dramatically symbolic of the complete collapse of the enemy, is not a vital part of the operation.

The embarkation of the troops and the preliminary air and naval preparations are proceeding according to schedule. I repeat that I and all of my commanders and staff officers, without exception, are enthusiastic for and confident of the success of the enveloping movement.

After dispatching my reply, I waited with growing concern an answer. Was it possible, I asked myself, that even now, when it was all but impossible to bring this great movement grinding to a halt, timidity in an office thousands of miles away, even if by a President himself, could stop this golden opportunity to turn defeat into victory? Finally, a short cryptic message arrived from the Joint Chiefs of Staff, announcing that in view of my reply they had approved the operation and "so informed the President." I interpreted this to mean that it had been the President who had threatened to interfere and overrule, on a professional military problem, his military advisers.

On September 12, 1950,

I boarded the *Mount McKinley* at Sasebo. A typhoon was blowing and we were hit with its full force. The second day out, the seas smoothed, the weather became bright and clear, and we headed for our rendezvous with the rest of the assault fleet. That evening I stood at the rail of the *Mount McKinley* and watched the sun go down beyond China over the horizon. I had made many landings before, but this was the most intricately complicated amphibious operation I had ever attempted. Next morning we would have to thread our way over the shifting bars of "Flying Fish Channel," under the guns of Wolmi-do, and skirt the edges of the deadly mud banks that stretched for 2 miles across the harbor.

All over the ship the tension that had been slowly building up since our departure was now approaching its climax. Even the Yellow Sea rushing past the ship's sides seemed to bespeak the urgency of our mission. That night, about half past two, I took a turn around the deck. The ship was blacked out from stem to stern. At their posts and battle stations the crew members were alert

American GI
returning from front.

and silent, no longer exchanging the customary banter. At the bow I stood listening to the rush of the sea and watched the fiery sparklets of phosphorescence as the dark ship plowed toward the target, the armada of other craft converging on the same area, all now past the point of no return. Within five hours, 40,000 men would act boldly, in the hope that 100,000 others manning the thin defense lines in South Korea would not die. I alone was responsible for tomorrow, and if I failed, the dreadful results would rest on judgment day against my soul.

Then I noticed a flash—a light that winked on and off across the water. The channel navigation lights were on. We were taking the enemy by surprise. The lights were not even turned off. I went to my cabin and turned in.

I could not have been asleep more than a couple of hours when a sudden thunder woke me. Our guns had opened up on Wolmi-do. I went to the bridge. This harbor island was now rocking under the bombardment of naval guns and aerial bombs. As I watched, blue Corsairs swooped down from the clouds and added their strafing to the destruction. Wreaths of dirty gray smoke were rising. Against this falling curtain the arching, fiery trails of thousands of rockets could be seen as they streaked toward Inchon's beaches. Immense explosions were erupting all along the shores. The endless circles of little landing craft churned around and around the mother assault ships.

The guns on Wolmi-do were silenced, and the first assault waves were going in. If the Marines who were leading were beaten off or even pinned down for too long, it would mean the enemy was in force. It would take only a few defenders to slaughter that first wave of invaders while the rest were held back by the enormous mud banks. At 8 A.M. an orderly climbs up to the bridge and hands me a slip of paper. It says the first wave of Marines have landed and secured a beachhead without a single fatality. I turned to Admiral Doyle and said: "Please send this message to the fleet: 'The Navy and the Marines have never shone more brightly than this morning.' Let's go down and have breakfast."

By the time the tide had gone out of Inchon's harbor, only an hour later, leaving some of the landing craft squatting on the mud banks, Wolmi-do had been fully secured. And late that afternoon, as soon as the tides rolled back in, I climbed into the gig of Admiral Struble and we went in to oversee the operation. At Wolmi-do I found that the enemy had started an intense fortification of the island. Had I listened to those who had wanted to delay the landing until the next high tides, nearly a month later, Wolmi-do would have been an impregnable fortress.

I directed the prompt seizure of Seoul to be followed by an advance toward the south. This would place the bulk of the enemy's army between the two giant prongs of my forces—the X Corps from the north, the Eighth Army from the south. This would forge the pincers, both the anvil and the hammer, for the stroke of complete annihilation of the North Korean armies.

The X Corps moved inland rapidly. One column headed for Seoul with the immediate mission to cut communications to the south and to seize Kimpo Airfield, the largest in all Korea. This would sever the jugular vein of the enemy. The other column moved on toward Suwon, its mission being to recapture the air base there and to move on as the northern area of the pincer movement. Events moved with great rapidity. Kimpo Airfield was captured, and signs of weakness began to be evident in front of Walker. I directed him to attack, and he promptly crossed the Naktong River in savage assault. The enemy resisted desperately, but with his supplies gone, caught between the pincers, and without retreat routes available, he gave way at an accelerated rate. Precipitate withdrawal carried him rapidly northward over 70 miles. Soon, complete disintegration set in. He was cut off from supply, command, and communications. Red regiments ceased to exist as organized units. Arms and equipment were abandoned; tanks, artillery, mortars, and small arms littered the highways and trails. Prisoners surrendered or were captured by the thousands. Within a month, the total of Red captives rose to 130,000. The enemy fought fiercely for Seoul, but by September 28th it had been cleared.

I moved at once to have the government of Korea re-established in Seoul. But at this juncture I received an astonishing message from Washington. In an order, undoubtedly instigated by the State Department, and reflecting its antagonism toward President Rhee, the Joint Chiefs of Staff admonished me that any plan for the restoration of his government "must have the approval of higher authority."

I replied instantly:

Your message is not understood. I have no plan

Visiting a command post
on the road to Yongdung-Po.

whatsoever except scrupulously to implement the directives I have received. These directives envision support of the resolutions of the United Nations Security Council of 25 and 27 June, calling upon member governments to furnish "such assistance to the Republic of Korea as may be necessary to repel the armed attacks and to restore international peace and security in the area."

The existing government of the Republic has never ceased to function. The position of the United States is stated in your message of July 7, Government of Republic of Korea is recognized by U.S. as responsible governing authority and only lawful government in Korea and is only Korean government whose legality has been recognized by U.N. authority; with the concurrence of the cabinet, senior members of the legislature, the United Nations Commission, and perhaps other or similar official, it will domicile in Seoul as soon as conditions there are sufficiently stable to permit reasonable security. This of course involves no reestablishment of government, nor indeed any change in government to its constitutional tion of the existing government to its constitutional seat in order to facilitate the resumption of the civil process, and to promote prompt and effective restoration of law and order in areas liberated from enemy control. Such action is not only very much desired by the American Ambassador and all others concerned, but appears to be implicit in my directives.

I ordered that on September 29th the city of Seoul be formally restored as the seat of the existing government.

At the capital building I pinned the Distinguished Service Cross on General Walker and General Almond, citing them for their marked skill and courage in exploiting the decisive pincer movement of Inchon. The scene was impressive as the ceremony of handing back the capital city began. In the war-shattered assembly room sat row on row of heavily armed officers and men of both the U.N. and R.O.K. armies. On both sides of the room, the windows gaped brokenly, and the smell of death drifted through them. My thoughts went back to that day in Malacanan Palace in Manila when I handed the seat of government over to the authorities of the Philippines. I asked that all present rise and join me in reciting the Lord's Prayer. The steel helmets and mud-caked fatigue caps came off as everyone rose to his feet. Together we recited the Lord's Prayer, and I remember particles of glass tinkling down from the shattered roof of the assembly room as I concluded, ". . . Thine is the Kingdom, the Power and the Glory, for ever and ever, Amen."

I began to have misgivings as to the concepts

by higher authority regarding the future of Korea. The golden moment to transmute our victory at Inchon into a political peace had arrived. Yet, it appeared that diplomatic inertia had set in, and we were failing to grasp the possibilities of ending the war and moving toward a decisive peace in the Pacific. The rule of the day was timidity and appeasement, which would not end the war, but increase the military efforts against us. I discussed my fears with General Walker, who agreed completely.

When, after Inchon, no diplomatic action looking toward peace seemed to be forthcoming, diverse views began to appear among the members of the United Nations. The United States took the position that if the North Korean Army was not completely destroyed, and peace and order restored in the northern half of the peninsula, South Korea would live indefinitely beneath the threat of renewed Communist aggression. Many others, led by the British, were opposed to sending United Nations Forces into North Korea. Their argument seemed to be that more could be accomplished in Asia by appeasement than by moral resolution. They seemed to believe that the leaders of Communism would temporize too, that they would upset the grand Communist design of eventual world domination, and follow a policy of expediency rather than long-range planning. A worldwide public debate erupted whether or not United Nations troops should cross the 38th Parallel to mop up the shattered remnants of the armed forces of North Korea. If not, would North Korea, behind the sanctuary of the 38th Parallel, be permitted to organize, train, and equip another army ready for battle?

The Joint Chiefs of Staff settled the question. Late in September, they sent me what they called "amplifying instructions as to further military action to be taken by you in Korea." These instructions stated unequivocally:

"Your military objective is the destruction of the North Korean armed forces. In attaining this objective, you are authorized to conduct military operations north of the 38th parallel in Korea. Under no circumstances, however, will your forces, ground, air or sea, cross the Manchurian or U.S.S.R. borders of Korea and, as a matter of policy, no non-Korean ground forces will be used in the North East provinces bordering the Soviet Union, or in the areas along the Manchurian border. Furthermore, support of your operations, north or south of the 38th parallel, will not include air

or naval action against Manchuria or against U.S.S.R. territory. When organized armed resistance by the North Korean Forces has been brought substantially to an end, you should direct the R.O.K. forces to take the lead in disarming remaining North Korean units and enforcing the terms of surrender. Circumstances obtaining at the time will determine the character of occupation of North Korea. Your plans for such an occupation will be forwarded for approval to the Joint Chiefs of Staff."

I replied:

"Briefly, my plan is: (a) Eighth Army as now constituted will attack across the 38th parallel with its main effort on the Pyongyang axis with the objective of seizing Pyongyang; (b) X Corps as now constituted will effect amphibious landing at Wonsan, making juncture with the Eighth Army; (c) 3rd Infantry Division will remain in Japan in GHQ reserve initially; (d) R.O.K. Army forces only will conduct operation north of the line Chungjo-Yongwon-Hungnan; (e) tentative date for the attack of the Eighth Army will not be earlier than 15 October and not later than 30 October."

On September 30th, the Joint Chiefs of Staff officially approved the plan. And six days later, their approval was confirmed by a resolution of the United Nations General Assembly. Later statements which flooded the newsstands of the world that the purpose of the United Nations was merely to drive the enemy across the 38th parallel and that I had gone beyond my authority in crossing the 38th parallel were pure fiction.

This decision presented me with problems of the gravest import. It immediately raised the shadow of Red Chinese intervention. Actually, the possibility of such an intervention had existed ever since the order from Washington, issued to the Seventh Fleet in June, to neutralize Formosa, which in effect protected the Red China mainland from attack by Chiang Kai-shek's force of half a million men. This released the two great Red Chinese armies assigned to the coastal defense of central China and made them available for transfer elsewhere. They were reported to be moving north toward Manchuria. It was undoubtedly this concept of sanctuary which tipped the scales in Red China's future decisions. Red China would represent for me new conditions and a totally new war. The United Nations chose to ignore this uncomfortable problem. No means were ever furnished or even considered to meet it, although the sinister implications were perfectly understood by all governments concerned. Unquestionably the failure, through inertia, of our diplomacy to utilize the victory of Inchon as the basis for swift and dynamic action to restore peace and unity to Korea was one of the greatest contributing causes to the subsequent war initiated by Red China.

On October 1st, in the hope of terminating the struggle, I called upon the commander-in-chief of the North Korean forces to cease hostilities "in order that the decisions of the United Nations may be carried out without further loss of life and destruction of property." I stipulated that "North Korean forces, including prisoners of war in the hands of the United Nations Command, will continue to be given the care dictated by civilized custom and practice and permitted to return to their homes." I received no response.

The Eighth Army then pressed rapidly forward toward Pyongyang, while the X Corps landed at Wonsan. The supply situation at Seoul was insufficient to maintain both the Eighth Army and the X Corps, and it was essential to establish a new port of supply entrance on the east coast. Due to tide difficulties at Inchon, where only 5,000 tons a day could be landed, and the destruction of the railroad from Pusan to Seoul during the campaign, limiting overland transportation to a minimum, Wonsan was selected as the new supply base. Tactically, it could bring flank pressure if necessary, for the capture of Pyongyang. It was essential also to secure the eastern corridor of the peninsula.

The so-called "waistline" between the east and west coasts of Korea is cut by a spinal mountain range which renders lateral communication extremely difficult between the two coastal areas, and the movement of supplies across the peninsula completely unpredictable. It was essential to secure both areas thus separated by the mountainous divide, as otherwise the entire eastern sector of the peninsula would have been left unguarded against an enemy flanking movement to the southeast, and the entire northeastern section of the peninsula would have been left open for maneuver against the Eighth Army's right. The terrain was such that there was little prospect that an enemy might drive an effective wedge between the two forces and initiate flanking operations against either or both, and no such attempt was ever made. Both the Eighth Army and the X Corps were under direct control and central co-

ordination of general headquarters until they were to meet in the north, when the united command would pass to General Walker. Until these two forces could unite, it would have been impossible for Walker in the west area to attempt command responsibility and co-ordination of the east coastal area. The logistical maintenance of an entirely separate and different supply line from Japan to the east coast would have been beyond him.

On October 9th, I addressed the head of the North Korean government, inviting attention to a resolution by the United Nations General Assembly, passed the day before, "to ensure conditions of stability throughout Korea" and to take "all constituent acts, including the holding of elections, under the auspices of the United Nations for the establishment of a unified, independent and democratic government in the sovereign state of Korea."

I called "upon all North Koreans to cooperate fully with the United Nations, assured that they would be treated justly and that the United Nations would act to relieve and rehabilitate all parts of a unified Korea." My summons was ignored.

On October 12th, I received two messages, one from Averell Harriman, the other from Secretary of Defense Marshall. Harriman's read: "I am looking forward keenly to seeing you shortly and to expressing to you personally my profound admiration for your magnificent campaign. Warm regards."

The other stated that President Truman would like to have a conference with me. The President suggested Honolulu on the 15th, but "if the situation in Korea is such that you feel you should not absent yourself for the time involved in such a long trip, I am sure the President would be glad to go on and meet you at Wake Island."

I replied: "I would be delighted to meet the President on the morning of the 15th at Wake Island."

I knew nothing of the purpose of the meeting, my only information being that Averell Harriman would be there. A number of American correspondents in Tokyo requested permission to accompany me. In view of the number of Washington correspondents announced as coming, I assumed that the Tokyo representatives would be permitted to attend also, especially as my plane could accommodate a large representation. I passed their requests along to the Pentagon, recommending approval, and was surprised when the request was promptly and curtly disapproved.

Facing page, top:
South Koreans clearing
the debris from their homes
after an attack from the North.

Facing page, bottom:
American-trained ROK soldier
guards Communist-led North Korean
captives near Seoul.

Above:
With Courtney Whitney,
General MacArthur's aide.

Below:
Meeting with President Truman
at Wake Island.

The President's party arrived in three planes with thirty-five reporters and photographers. As I shook hands with Mr. Truman, he remarked, "I've been a long time meeting you, General."

I replied, "I hope it won't be so long next time." But there was never to be a next time.

I had been warned about Mr. Truman's quick and violent temper and prejudices, but he radiated nothing but courtesy and good humor during our meeting. He has an engaging personality, a quick and witty tongue, and I liked him from the start. At the conference itself, he seemed to take great pride in his historical knowledge, but, it seemed to me that in spite of his having read much, it was of a superficial character, encompassing facts without the logic and reasoning dictating those facts. Of the Far East he knew little, presenting a strange combination of distorted history and vague hopes that somehow, some way, we could do something to help those struggling against Communism.

His advisers were numerous and distinguished: Admiral Arthur Radford, commander of the Pacific Fleet; Army Secretary Frank Pace; Press Secretary Charles Ross; U.N. Ambassador Philip Jessup; Joint Chiefs Chairman Omar Bradley; State Department Far Eastern Chief Dean Rusk; Special Adviser Averell Harriman; and Legal Adviser Charles Murphy. There were numerous other Truman aides and aides' aides. I had with me my military secretary, my aide-de-camp, and my pilot. Press Secretary Ross announced that no record was to be made of the talks.

Wake Island's heat caused the President to remove his coat. I pulled out a new briar pipe and inquired: "Do you mind if I smoke, Mr. President?"

Truman replied, "No. I suppose I've had more smoke blown in my face than any other man alive." He seemed to enjoy the laugh that followed.

The conference itself was innocuous enough. The sketchy agenda contained nothing upon which Washington did not already have my fullest views as they affected my responsibilities either as supreme commander for the Allied powers in Japan or as commander-in-chief for the United Nations in Korea. They dealt with such matters as the administration of Korea when united, its rehabilitation, the treatment of prisoners of war, the economic situation in the Philippines, the security of Indo-China, the progress of a treaty of peace with Japan, routine details of supply logistics for Japan and Korea—nothing on which my views were not known. No new policies, no new strategy of war or international politics, were proposed or discussed. Formosa was not on the agenda.

Near the end of the conference, the possibility of Chinese intervention was brought up almost casually. It was the general consensus of all present that Red China had no intention of intervening. This opinion had previously been advanced by the Central Intelligence Agency and the State Department. General Bradley went so far as to bring up the question of transferring troops in the Far East to Europe, and said he would like to have two divisions from Korea home by Christmas for this purpose.

My views were asked as to the chance of Red China's intervention. I replied that the answer could only be speculative; that neither the State Department through its diplomatic listening posts abroad, nor the Central Intelligence Agency to whom a field commander must look for guidance as to a foreign nation's intention to move from peace to war, reported any evidence of intent by the Peiping government to intervene with major forces; that my own local intelligence, which I regarded as unsurpassed anywhere, reported heavy concentrations near the Yalu border in Manchuria whose movements were indeterminate; that my own military estimate was that with our largely unopposed air forces, with their potential capable of destroying, at will, bases of attack and lines of supply north as well as south of the Yalu, no Chinese military commander would hazard the commitment of large forces upon the devastated Korean peninsula. The risk of their utter destruction through lack of supply would be too great. There was no disagreement from anyone. This episode was later completely misrepresented to the public through an alleged but spurious report in an effort to pervert the position taken by me. It was an ingeniously fostered implication that I flatly and unequivocally predicted that under no circumstances would the Chinese Communists enter the Korean War. This is prevarication.

At the airstrip, Truman surprised me by stepping up to the microphones that had been set up by the newsreel photographers, and reading to the assemblage that had gathered, a citation awarding me, by the President of the United States, the Distinguished Service Medal.

The conference at Wake Island made me realize that a curious, and sinister, change was taking place in Washington. The defiant, rallying figure

Watching paratroopers descend behind North Korean lines.

that had been Franklin Roosevelt was gone. Instead, there was a tendency toward temporizing rather than fighting it through. The original courageous decision of Harry Truman to boldly meet and defeat Communism in Asia was apparently being chipped away by the constant pounding whispers of timidity and cynicism. The President seemed to be swayed by the blandishments of some of the more selfish politicians of the United Nations. He seemed to be in the anomalous position of openly expressing fears of over-calculated risks that he had fearlessly taken only a few months before.

This put me as field commander in an especially difficult situation. Up to now I had been engaged in warfare as it had been conducted through the ages—to fight to win. But I could see now that the Korean War was developing into something quite different. There seemed to be a deliberate under-estimating of the importance of the conflict to which the government had committed—and was expending—the lives of United States fighting men.

What had been the purpose of the conference was difficult to diagnose. Many regarded it as largely a political gimmick. The Congressional elections were but two weeks away, and in this way the President could identify his party with the favorable results of the Inchon victory. Such reasoning, I am sure, does Mr. Truman an injustice. I believe nothing of the sort animated him, and that the sole purpose was to create good will and beneficial results to the country. My opinion along this line was strengthened by the letter he wrote me in longhand on his return to Washington. It read:

The meeting at Wake Island was a most satisfying one to me. I was pleased with the chance to meet and talk to you about Japan, Korea, and other Far Eastern countries. I was happy to have your views on all the Asiatic situations with which we are faced.

Our meeting has had a splendid reaction here in the United States, and I think it was well worthwhile if for no other reason than that we became personally acquainted.

Sincerely

I replied in part:

I left the Wake Island conference with a distinct sense of satisfaction that the country's interests had been well served through the better mutual understanding and exchange of views which it afforded. I hope that it will result in building a strong defense against future efforts of those who seek for one reason or another, none of them worthy, to breach the understanding between us.

With expressions of deep respect.

But my hope was futile. Propaganda and prejudice reigned supreme.

On October 20th, 1950,

the Eighth Army hit Pyongyang. The ground troops assaulted from the south and a parachute drop by the 187th Regimental Combat Team 25 miles north of the city completed its envelopment. The move was almost a duplicate of the one that "closed the gap" at Nadzab, in New Guinea. I watched the capture of the city from my plane, which then landed me on its spacious airfield.

Pyongyang was the enemy's capital, and its fall symbolized the complete defeat of North Korea. Practically all organized resistance came to an end, leaving only a type of guerrilla warfare in its place. Aggressive Communism had been decisively defeated at a time and place of its own choosing. The prestige of the United Nations, and especially the United States, was again high in all of Asia.

But at Pyongyang, both General Walker and myself were greatly disturbed by the supply situation which faced the Eighth Army. Supply is the nerve system of any military operation. The rail lines from Pusan, our naval base for overseas deliveries, had been thoroughly worked over by our air force during the months of our perimeter defense. The port of Inchon, the sea harbor of Seoul, was restricted by the same adverse tidal conditions which had aroused such violent opposition to our initial amphibious attack there. The port of Chinnampo, the sea harbor of Pyongyang, had a very limited capacity. The net result of all these adverse logistical factors was materially to slow down the advance northward. We were worried, too, by the growing indication of a startling build-up of Red Chinese troops in Manchuria, just north of the Yalu.

I was even more worried by a series of directives from Washington which were greatly decreasing the potential of my air force. First I was forbidden "hot" pursuit of enemy planes that attacked our own. Manchuria and Siberia were sanctuaries of inviolate protection for all enemy forces and for all enemy purposes, no matter what depredations or assaults might come from there.

Then I was denied the right to bomb the hydro-electric plants along the Yalu. The order was broadened to include every plant in North Korea which was capable of furnishing electric power to Manchuria and Siberia. Most incomprehensible of all was the refusal to let me bomb the important supply center at Racin, which was not in Manchuria or Siberia, but many miles from the border, in northeast Korea. Racin was a depot to which the Soviet Union forwarded supplies from Vladivostok for the North Korean Army. I felt that step-by-step my weapons were being taken away from me.

Leading elements of the X Corps reached the Yalu River by November 21st, but General Walker began to experience difficulties. His report to me stated:

The Eighth Army was advancing on a broad front in widely separated columns in pursuit of the defeated North Korean forces. The advance north from Pyongyang was based on a calculated logistical risk involving supply almost entirely by airlift. Available supplies were sufficient only for bare maintenance of combat operations against light opposition, with no possibility of accumulating reserves to meet heavier opposition. An enemy attack against the II South Korean Corps threw it into confusion and halted the advance. There is no intention to take up or remain on the defense. Every effort is being made to retain an adequate bridgehead to facilitate the resumption of the attack as soon as conditions permit. All units continue to execute local attack. Plans have been prepared for resumption of the offensive to meet the new factor of organized Chinese Communist forces. These plans will be put into execution at the earliest possible moment.

The most disquieting feature of the situation was the indication that an estimated three fresh divisions, apparently consisting of Red Chinese troops, had joined the battle. The obvious questions began to assume significance. Was this a Red Chinese reconnaissance in force made across the Yalu as a defensive maneuver to obtain information of Eighth Army intentions? Was it the commitment of fresh North Korean units organized, trained, and equipped in Manchuria with a sprinkling of Chinese "volunteers"? Was it merely Red bluff? Or did it represent the jabs of a full-scale Red Chinese offensive?

The Red Chinese government had a ready explanation for the situation, which it announced to the world—the Chinese in North Korea were merely individual volunteers who had gone to the assistance of their Korean comrades. I brushed aside this subterfuge and reported to Washington: "Recent captures of soldiers of Chinese nationality and information obtained from their interrogations, together with increased resistance being encountered by United Nations forces, remove the problem of Chinese intervention from the realm of the academic, and turns it into a serious immediate threat." I felt that I could not ignore the assumption that Red China had determined upon a commitment of some kind, and at the same time I certainly could not yet assume from the evidence at hand that the decision had been made in Peiping for all-out war in Korea. The logical source for information on any such policy decisions made in Peiping was, of course, Washington, and not the front line in Korea. But neither through the State Department, the Defense Department, the Central Intelligence Agency, nor even the United Nations neutrals, who usually professed authoritative knowledge of the goings-on inside China, was there any reliable or useful knowledge on the subject. I was left in a No-Man's Land of indecision.

On November 3rd, I furnished Washington a Communist battle order, listing in complete numerical detail strength and locations in Manchuria of fifty-six regular army divisions, in sixteen corps —a total of 498,000 men. In addition, there were district service forces of 370,000, or an aggregate of 868,000 in all. Meanwhile, other forces were still converging northward from central China. This intelligence was furnished not only to Washington, but to the United Nations, either of whom could have stopped our troops at any point in North Korea if they had taken the mounting Chinese threat seriously. But the order I received was:

In the event of the open or covert employment anywhere in Korea of major Chinese Communist units, without prior announcement, you should continue the action as long as, in your judgment, action by forces now under your control offers a reasonable chance of success. In any case, prior to taking any military action against objectives in Chinese territory, you will obtain authorization from Washington.

I tried to arouse higher authority to the emergency by attempting to explain to Washington

the aggressive belligerency of the Chinese—their activities in Korea have been offensive, never defensive. In order to understand their motivating influences, one must examine the changes in Chinese character and culture. Up until fifty years ago, China was decompartmented into groups divided against each other. Their war-making tendency was almost non-existent. Not until the turn of the century did China's nationalist urge begin. This was further developed under the leadership of Chiang Kai-shek, but has been brought to its greatest fruition under the present regime, to the point that it has now taken on the character of a united nationalism of increasingly dominant aggressive tendencies.

Through these past fifty years the Chinese people have thus become militarized in their concepts and in their ideals. They now make first class soldiers and are developing competent commanders and staffs. This has produced a new and dominant power in Asia, which for its own purposes has allied with Soviet Russia, but which in its own concepts and methods has become aggressively imperialistic, with a lust for expansion and increased power normal to this type of imperialism.

There is little of the ideological either one way or the other in the Chinese makeup. The standard of living is so low, and the capital accumulation has been so thoroughly dissipated by war, that the masses are desperate and avid to follow any leadership which seems to promise alleviation of local stringencies. I have from the beginning believed that the Chinese Communists' support of the North Koreans was the dominant one. Their interests at present are parallel to those of the Soviet, but I believe that the aggressiveness now displayed, not only in Korea but in Indo-China, and Tibet pointing toward the south, reflects predominantly the same lust for the expansion of power which has animated every would-be conqueror since the beginning of time.

Quezon once said to me in the darkest days of Bataan, "I have no fear that we will not ultimately defeat the Japanese, nor do I feel any dread of ultimate conquest by them. My great fear is the Chinese. With their increasing militarism and aggressive tendency, they are the great Asiatic menace. They have no real ideologies, and when they reach the fructification of their military potential, I dread to think what may happen."

At this time such confusion existed in the public mind, due to biased and misleading news accounts, that I felt a clear explanation of the situation at hand was needed in order that both the American people and the peoples of the other United Nations, whose troops were fighting under my command, would understand what confronted their soldiers, sailors, marines, and airmen. I therefore issued a special communique on November 6th.

The Korean War was brought to a practical end with the closing of the trap on enemy elements north of Pyongyang and seizure of the east coastal area,

*Above and
following pages:*
**Preparing for U.N. offensive
against the North Koreans.**

resulting in raising the number of enemy prisoners-of-war in our hands to well over 135,000 which, with other losses mounting to over 200,000, brought enemy casualties to above 335,000, representing a fair estimate of North Korean total military strength. The defeat of the North Koreans and destruction of their armies was thereby decisive. In the face of this victory for United Nations arms, the Communists, without any notice of belligerency, moved elements of Chinese Communist forces across the Yalu River into North Korea and massed a great concentration of possible reinforcing divisions, with adequate supply behind the privileged sanctuary of the adjacent Manchurian border. The present situation therefore is this: While the North Korean forces with which we were initially engaged have been destroyed or rendered impotent for military action, a new and fresh army faces us, backed up by a possibility of large reserves and adequate supplies within easy reach of the enemy but beyond the limits of our present sphere of military action. Whether, and to what extent these reserves will be moved forward remains to be seen and is a matter of gravest international significance. Our present mission is limited to the destruction of those forces now arrayed against us in North Korea with a view to achieving the United Nations' objective to bring unity and peace to the Korean nation and people.

Despite the welter of restrictions placed upon me by Washington, I felt there remained one weapon I could use against massive Chinese intervention. I ordered General Stratemeyer to employ ninety B-29's on the following morning to destroy the Yalu bridges and cut this easy line of communication between Manchuria and North Korea, over which large armies of Chinese Reds could swarm. Up to now I had avoided doing so because of the danger of accidentally missing the targets and dropping bombs in Manchuria, which had been forbidden.

An immediate dispatch came from Secretary Marshall countermanding my order and directing me "to postpone all bombing of targets within five miles of the Manchurian border." It seemed to me incredible that protection should be extended to the enemy, not only of the bridges which were the only means they had for moving their men and supplies across that wide natural river barrier into North Korea, but also for a 5-mile-deep area on this side of the Yalu in which to establish a bridgehead. It would be impossible to exaggerate my astonishment, and I at once protested.

I called attention to my previous warnings that there was a substantial movement across the bridges.

The only way to stop this reinforcement of the enemy is the destruction of the bridges by air attack and air destruction of installations in North Korea which would facilitate the movement. I feel that the operation is within the scope of the rules of war and the resolutions and directives which I have received. And I can accept the instructions rescinding my orders only under the greatest protest, as I feel that they might well result in a calamity of gravest proportions, for which I could not accept the responsibility. Urgently request reconsideration of your decision, or that the matter be brought to the attention of the President for his review.

All that resulted was a modification of the order to permit the bombing of the "Korean end of the Yalu bridges."

I asked Stratemeyer to study the conditions under which the bombing of the Yalu bridges was to be permitted. He reported: "It cannot be done—Washington must have known it cannot be done."

The head of the Far East Bomber Command, Major General Emmett (Rosey) O'Donnell, made the following estimate of the situation:

We were not allowed to violate Manchurian territory, and by violation of the territory I mean we were not allowed to fly over an inch of it. For instance, like most rivers, the Yalu has several pronounced bends before getting to the town of Antung, and the main bridges at Antung we had to attack in only one manner—in order not to violate Manchurian territory, and that was a course tangential to the southernmost bend of the river. As you draw a line from the southernmost bend of the river to the bridge, that is your course. These people on the other side of the river knew that and put up their batteries right along the line, and they peppered us right down the line all the way. We had to take it, of course, and couldn't fight back. In addition to that, they had their fighters come up alongside and join our formation about two miles to the lee and fly along at the same speed on the other side of the river while we were making our approach. And just before we got to bomb-away position, they would veer off to the north and climb up to about 30,000 feet and then make a frontal quarter attack on the bombers just about at the time of bomb-away in a turn. So they would be coming from Manchuria in a turn, swoop down, fire their cannons at the formation, and continue to turn back to sanctuary.

One of those bomber pilots, wounded unto death, the stump of an arm dangling by his side, gasped at me through the bubbles of blood he spat out, "General, which side are Washington and the United Nations on?" It seared my very soul.

I at once asked for immediate relief from as-

signment to duty in the Far East. In my bitterness I told my able Chief of Staff, General Doyle Hickey:

For the first time in military history, a commander has been denied the use of his military power to safeguard the lives of his soldiers and safety of his army. To me it clearly foreshadows a future tragic situation in the Far East and leaves me with a sense of inexpressible shock. It will cost the lives of thousands of American soldiers and place in jeopardy the entire army. By some means the enemy commander must have known of this decision to protect his lines of communication into North Korea, or he never would have dared to cross those bridges in force.

Hickey protested that the army would not understand my leaving at such a critical moment, and might become demoralized and destroyed; that it was my duty to the country and to my own honor not to go at such a crisis. I tore up my dispatch. It is interesting to know that several years later General Eisenhower was reported in the press to have said that had he been in my place and received such an order, he would have ignored it. That would have at least assured his immediate relief from command.

On the day following this extraordinary directive, and my protest, Secretary Marshall sent me a message conciliatory in tone which stated that my concern over the alarming developments was shared by the authorities in Washington. Truman was vacationing at this time in his home in Missouri. Marshall said:

The discussions and decisions here are heavily weighted with the extremely delicate situation we have before the Security Council of the United Nations, whose meeting tomorrow may have fateful consequences. We all realize your difficulty in fighting a desperate battle in a mountainous region under winter conditions and with a multinational force in all degrees of preparedness. I also understand, I think, the difficulty involved in conducting such a battle under necessarily limited conditions and the necessity of keeping the distant headquarters, in Washington, informed of developments and decisions. However, this appears to be unavoidable. We are faced with an extremely grave international problem.

I could not have agreed more that the situation in Korea was fraught with disaster. The danger was that by meeting naked force with appeasement we would not only perpetrate military disaster in Korea, but would enable Communism to make its bid for most of Asia. This was a far larger, more complex, long-range problem than

Above:
Preparing for U.N. offensive.

Right:
At a press conference somewhere in Korea.

Washington seemed to comprehend.

At about this time, the British Labour government suggested a strange solution to the problem of combating Red Chinese intervention—give the Communists a slice of North Korea to serve as a "buffer" area and as evidence of the United Nations' good intentions.

In protesting the short-sightedness of the British proposal, I compared it with the ceding of the Sudetenland to Germany in 1938. Besides violating the spirit of the United Nations decision of June 25th, this so-called "buffer" zone would be a signal to further aggression on the part of the Chinese, and perhaps most important, would bankrupt our political, military, and psychological position in the Far East.

There were but three possible courses. I could go forward, remain immobile, or withdraw. If I went forward, there was the chance that China might not intervene in force and the war would be over. If I remained immobile and waited, it would be necessary to select a defense line and dig in. But there was no terrain with natural obstacles to take advantage of, and with my scant forces it would be impossible to establish a defense in depth against the overwhelming numbers of Chinese. They had enough divisions to surround the army if it remained stationary, and every day they would increase their force by fresh divisions from Manchuria. This would mean the ultimate annihilation of our entire command. I estimated our forces would have to be at least tripled to cope with such a situation, but no promise of reinforcements by Washington was forthcoming. If the Chinese intended to intervene, this is exactly what they would want me to do. If I withdrew, it would be in contradiction to my orders and would destroy any opportunity to bring the Korean War to a successful end.

If I went forward and found the Chinese in force, my strategy would be to immediately break contact and withdraw rapidly, so as to lengthen and expose the enemy's supply lines. This would result in a pyramiding of logistical difficulties for the Reds and an almost astronomical increase in the destructiveness of our air power. Every step forward, his strength would decrease as compared with mine, until a degree of parity would be reached between the opposing forces. I would then rely upon maneuver, with my objective his supply lines. I would withdraw the X Corps to Pusan by sea when it had completed its covering of the right flank of the Eighth Army, build up my communications northward, and estimate the new situation that would develop.

I reviewed my orders from Washington: "In the event of the open or covert employment anywhere in Korea of major Chinese Communist units, without prior announcement, you should continue the action as long as, in your judgment, action by forces now under your control offers a reasonable chance of success." I concluded that the best "posture of security" was to go forward. This would deny the enemy the selection of the time and place of his attack, and the accumulation of additional forces from Manchuria. It would be simultaneously a mopping-up of the defeated North Korean forces, and a reconnaissance in force to probe the intentions of the Chinese. If our forward movement should prematurely expose Chinese involvement, my troops would have the necessary freedom of action to escape its jaws. In anticipation of such a situation, I directed Walker to prepare complete operational plans for disengagement and withdrawal from action in the event it developed that Red China was entering the Korean War in determined force. The field commander and staffs all agreed with my basic plan. It was submitted by me to, and approved by, the Joint Chiefs of Staff in Washington.

Meanwhile, behind the curtain of fright and frustration thrown up along the Yalu by Washington, the Chinese Communists, over a period of twenty days, were stealthily surging over the Yalu bridges into position for an attack. Under cover of darkness, and the deadly pattern of anti-aircraft defense permitted by the United Nations restrictions, they poured more than 200,000 fresh troops into North Korea between November 6th and November 26th. The order not to bomb the Yalu bridges was the most indefensible and ill-conceived decision ever forced on a field commander in our nation's history.

On November 24th, I flew to Eighth Army headquarters on the Chongchon River. Walker's advance had been originally set for November 15th, but supplies had not yet caught up, and the date had been postponed. The supply system was still unsatisfactory, but both Walker and myself felt we could wait no longer. Every day allowed more thousands to cross the Yalu bridges, and every day brought closer the winter weather, which would freeze the Yalu and let thousands more across. It was essential to move before Chinese superiority in numbers became overwhelming.

For five hours I toured our front lines. In talk-

ing to a group of officers, I told them of General Bradley's desire and hope to have two divisions home by Christmas provided there was not intervention by Red China. This remark was twisted by the press into a prediction of the success of our movement, and this false misinterpretation was later used as a powerful propaganda weapon with which to bludgeon me.

What I had seen at the front worried me greatly. The R.O.K. troops were not yet in good shape, and the entire line was deplorably weak in numbers. If the Chinese were actually in heavy force, I decided I would withdraw our troops at once and abandon any further attempt to move north. I decided to reconnoiter and try to see with my own eyes, and interpret with my own long experience what was going on behind the enemy's lines. I boarded my plane and instructed the pilot, Major Tony Story, to head for the mouth of the Yalu River. The plane was unarmed and would be an easy target for anti-aircraft fire or air interception, but I hoped that the very audacity of the flight would be its own protection.

When we reached the mouth of the Yalu, I told Story to turn east and follow the river at an altitude of 5,000 feet. At this height we could observe in detail the entire area of international No-Man's Land all the way to the Siberian border. All that spread before our eyes was an endless expanse of utterly barren countryside, jagged hills, yawning crevices, and the black waters of the Yalu locked in the silent death grip of snow and ice. It was a merciless wasteland. If a large force or massive supply train had passed over the border, the imprints had already been well-covered by the intermittent snowstorms of the Yalu Valley. I decided to have Walker await withdrawing until actual combat might indicate its necessity.

To my astonishment, I was awarded the Distinguished Flying Cross, and later the honorary wings of a combat pilot. The Air Force's partiality toward me is one of my most grateful memories.

On my return from the Eighth Army to headquarters, I found a message from the Joint Chiefs of Staff waiting for me. It said:

There is a growing concern within the United Nations over the possibility of bringing on a general conflict should a major clash develop with Chinese Communist forces as a result of your forces advancing squarely against the entire boundary between Korea and Manchuria. Proposals in United Nations may suggest unwelcome restrictions on your advance to the north. The consensus of political and military

Above: Marine guarding pass twelve miles north of Han Hung, Korea.
Below: With MacArthur are Major General Courtney Whitney (second from left) and Lieutenant General Matthew D. Ridgway during U.N. offensive.

opinion at a meeting held Thursday with the Secretaries of State and Defense, the Joint Chiefs of Staff and other officials, was that there should be no change in your mission, but that immediate action should be taken at top governmental level to formulate a course of action which will permit the establishment of a unified Korea and at the same time reduce risk of more general involvement.

Then came a suggestion that after advancing to a position near the Yalu, I should secure the position using R.O.K. forces to "hold the terrain dominating the approaches from the Valley of the Yalu." The limit of my advance in the northeast would be fixed at Chongjin. It went on to say: "Exploratory discussions were had to discover what military measures might lend themselves to political action which would reduce the tension with Peiping and the Soviet Union." I informed Washington that, in my opinion, we would never alter Chinese plans by being timid.

On November 27th, the Red commander, General Lin Piao, launched his full forces across the Yalu and into battle. Red China thus entered into open war against United States forces and those allied with us. Two Chinese Army Groups, the Fourth, operating against Walker, the Third, against Almond, attacked with overwhelming force.

The blow by the Fourth Army Group was on the South Korean II Corps, which broke, exposing the flank of the American Eighth Army troops. Walker immediately directed a rapid withdrawal, as had been planned. The 2nd Division and the Turkish contingent conducted notable rearguard actions which enabled the Eighth Army to break contact and avoid any enemy flanking movement.

The X Corps faced even greater odds than the Eighth Army. Almond, in accordance with instructions, withdrew toward Wonsan at once. The 1st Marine Division had been almost completely enveloped and had to fight its way back under its valiant commander, General Oliver Smith.

The withdrawal of both our forces was made with great skill. I regarded the professional part of the whole operation with the greatest satisfaction. I felt that the hard decisions I had been forced to make, and the skill displayed by my field commanders had saved the army. The movement north had upset the enemy's timetable, causing him to move prematurely, and to reveal the surreptitious massing of his armies. He had hoped to quietly assemble a massive force till spring, and destroy us with one mighty blow. Had I not acted when I did, we would have been a "sitting duck" doomed to eventual annihilation.

Our losses in the entire Yalu operations were comparatively light. In the Eighth Army, the number of troops killed, wounded, and missing amounted to 7,337, and in the X Corps to 5,638. This was about half the loss at Iwo Jima, less than one-fifth of that at Okinawa, and even less in comparison with the Battle of the Bulge.

That there was some leak in intelligence was evident to everyone. Walker continually complained to me that his operations were known to the enemy in advance through sources in Washington. I will always believe that if the United States had issued a warning to the effect that any entry of the Chinese Communists in force into Korea would be considered an act of international war against the United States, that the Korean War would have terminated with our advance north. I feel that the Reds would have stayed on their side of the Yalu. Instead, information must have been relayed to them, assuring that the Yalu bridges would continue to enjoy sanctuary and that their bases would be left intact. They knew they could swarm down across the Yalu River without having to worry about bombers hitting their Manchurian supply lines.

An official leaflet by General Lin Piao published in China read:

I would never have made the attack and risked my men and military reputation if I had not been assured that Washington would restrain General Mac-Arthur from taking adequate retaliatory measures against my lines of supply and communication.

I reported to the Joint Chiefs of Staff, advising that the Chinese military forces were committed in North Korea in great and ever-increasing strength. Interrogation of prisoners of war and other intelligence information established that exclusive of North Korean elements, the thirty-eighth, thirty-ninth, fortieth, forty-second, sixty-sixth, fiftieth, and twentieth Chinese Communist Field Armies were now in action. No pretext of minor support under the guise of volunteerism or other subterfuge had the slightest validity. We faced an entirely new war.

It was quite evident that our present strength was not sufficient to meet this undeclared war by the Chinese, especially with the advantages gained through our own timidity. The opportunity of initial onslaught in overwhelming force of undeclared belligerency, which so frequently occurred

in the past, is inherent in war itself. It could not be avoided under present conditions of international relationship. The resulting situation presented an entirely new picture which broadened the potentialities to world-embracing considerations beyond the sphere of decision by the theater commander. The issues must find their solution within the councils of the United Nations and chancelleries of the world. This command did everything humanly possible within its capabilities, but was now faced with conditions beyond its control and strength. The limitless capabilities of the entire Chinese nation, with Soviet logistical support, were arrayed against it. My strategic plan for the immediate future was to pass from the offensive to the defensive, with such local adjustments as may be required by a constantly fluid situation. The Joint Chiefs of Staff approved, and a new war thus started in Korea.

On November 29th, I wired Washington urgently recommending that "the theater commander be authorized to negotiate directly with the Chinese government authorities on Formosa for the movement north and incorporation into United Nations command of such Chinese units as may be available and desirable for reinforcing our position in Korea." My recommendation, Washington replied, was under consideration, but a firm answer would be delayed because it involved "world-wide consequences. We shall have to consider the possibility that it would disrupt the united position of the nations associated with us in the United Nations, and leave the United States isolated. It may be wholly unacceptable to the Commonwealth countries to have their forces employed with Nationalist China. Our position of leadership in the Far East is being most seriously compromised in the United Nations. The utmost care will be necessary to avoid the disruption of the essential Allied line-up in that organization."

Long after the event, some sources mistakenly tried to adduce additional reasons as to why Chiang Kai-shek's offer of help was not accepted. Spurious claims were made that the troops were of doubtful value, that not only were they overage and poorly trained, but they were untrustworthy and at the first contact with the Red Chinese would probably defect to the enemy. During my trip to Taiwan, I had an opportunity to observe troops of the Nationalist Army, and I gained the distinct impression that they were well-equipped and well-trained and of the same general quality as the soldiers of Red China. They were certainly trustworthy, free men in the Nationalist Army by choice, and would have been undoubtedly effective in battle. To the best of my knowledge, no one ever questioned this fact at the time.

United Nations member governments refused to consent to the use of the eager, fresh troops offered by Chiang Kai-shek, nor were sizeable reinforcements forthcoming from any other source. In a press conference, President Truman threatened once that he might make atomic weapons available to the United Nations command in this uneven battle, but within forty-eight hours Prime Minister Attlee hurried to Washington, and nothing more was heard of it. Actually, after the entry of China into the war, the American forces were compelled to face odds never before encountered in the military history of the nation. It is impossible to understand on a professional basis how we could have placidly accepted the disadvantages piled on the Eighth Army in Korea.

Early in January, I stabilized the lines of the Eighth Army at a position midway in South Korea. The progressive deterioration of the enemy's supply potential was working with deadly effect. Walker's skillful withdrawal had been accomplished with such speed that it led to many comments by ignorant correspondents that the troops were in flight. Nothing could have been further from the truth. The troops moved in good order and with unbroken cohesion among the various components. They were in excellent spirit and good condition.

As soon as the X Corps had completed its mission of protecting Walker's right flank from envelopment, I directed its withdrawal by sea to Pusan to join the Eighth Army. Almond's three divisions, the 1st Marine, 2nd and 7th Infantry, fought brilliant actions that stopped three Chinese corps in their tracks. The evacuation from Hungnan was a classic. General Almond's report on December 24th read:

The X Corps has completed evacuation by air and sea from Hungnan. 350,000 tons of supplies and equipment have been withdrawn. Nothing has been left to the enemy. 105,000 troops, including South Korean units and approximately 100,000 refugees, have been evacuated to safety in South Korea. Structures of possible military value to the enemy have been destroyed. The enemy paid heavily for his attempt to interfere with our operations. The losses of our forces were comparatively light.

When the X Corps arrived at Pusan, it was in excellent shape, with high morale and conspicuous self-confidence.

I myself felt we had reached up, sprung the Red trap, and escaped it. To have saved so many thousands of lives entrusted to my care gave me a sense of comfort that, in comparison, made all the honors I had ever received pale into insignificance.

The basic policies and decisions which had governed operations against the North Korean Army were still in effect, but the situation had entirely changed. This was a new war against the vast military potential of Red China. What I needed, as much as more men and arms and supplies, was a clear definition of policy to meet this new situation. Washington, however, again seemed uncertain and doubtful as to what course to pursue. I received this message from the Joint Chiefs of Staff:

It appears from all estimates available that the Chinese Communists possess the capability of forcing United Nations forces out of Korea if they choose to exercise it. The execution of this capability might be prevented by making the effort so costly to the enemy that they would abandon it, or by committing substantial additional United States forces to that theatre, thus seriously jeopardizing other commitments including the safety of Japan. It is not practical to obtain significant additional forces for Korea from other members of the United Nations. We believe that Korea is not the place to fight a major war. Further, we believe that we should not commit our remaining available ground forces to action against Chinese Communist forces in Korea in face of the increased threat of general war. However, a successful resistance to Chinese-North Korean aggression at some position in Korea and a deflation of the military and political prestige of the Chinese Communists would be of great importance to our national interest, if they could be accomplished without incurring serious losses.

Your basic directive required modification in the light of the present situation. You are now directed to defend in successive positions, subject to the primary consideration of the continued threat to Japan, and to determine in advance our last reasonable opportunity for an orderly evacuation. It seems to us that if you forced back to position in the vicinity of the Kum River a line generally eastward therefrom, and if thereafter the Chinese Communists mass large forces against your positions with an evident capability of forcing us out of Korea, it then would be necessary under these conditions to direct you to commence a withdrawal to Japan. Your views are requested as to the above outlined conditions which should determine a decision to initiate evacuation, particularly in the light of your continuing primary mission of defense of Japan, for which only troops of the Eighth Army are available.

This message seemed to indicate a loss of the "will to win" in Korea. President Truman's resolute determination to free and unite that threatened land had now deteriorated almost into defeatism. Washington planning was not directed toward methods of counterattack, but rather toward the best way to run; no solution was advanced as to the problem of reinforcement, even with Nationalist Chinese troops, but toward unrealistically expecting the impossible from men who had gone in to fight one war, had won it, and were now trying to fight a much bigger one. What seemed especially fantastic was to expect the Eighth Army, already facing a vastly superior Chinese force, to accept the additional responsibility, in case of Russian intervention, for the defense of Japan. The thought of defeat in Korea had never been entertained by me. It was my belief that, if allowed to use my full military might, without artificial restrictions, I could not only save Korea, but also inflict such a destructive blow upon Red China's capacity to wage aggressive war that it would remove her as a further threat to peace in Asia for generations to come.

Late in the evening of December 30th, I sat down to compose my reply to the Joint Chiefs of Staff's message on the evacuation of Korea.

Any estimate of relative capabilities in the Korean campaign appears to be dependent upon political-military policies yet to be formulated regarding Chinese military operations being conducted against our forces. It is quite clear now that the entire military resources of the Chinese nation, with logistic support from the Soviet, is committed to a maximum effort against the United Nations Command. In implementation of this commitment, a major concentration of Chinese forces in the Korean-Manchurian area will increasingly leave China vulnerable to areas from which troops to support Korean operations have been drawn. Meanwhile, under existing restrictions, our naval and air potential are being only partially utilized and the great potential of Chinese Nationalist force on Formosa and guerilla action on the mainland are being ignored. Indeed, as to the former, we are preventing its employment against the common enemy by our own naval force.

Should a policy determination be reached by our government or through it by the United Nations to recognize the state of war which has been forced upon us by the Chinese authorities and to take retaliatory measures within our capabilities, we could: (1)

blockade the coast of China; (2) destroy through naval gunfire and air bombardment China's industrial capacity to wage war; (3) secure reinforcements from the Nationalist garrison on Formosa to strengthen our position in Korea if we decided to continue the fight for that peninsula; and (4) release existing restrictions upon the Formosan garrison for diversionary action, possibly leading to counter-invasion against vulnerable areas of the Chinese mainland.

I believe that by the foregoing measures we could severely cripple and largely neutralize China's capability to wage aggressive war and thus save Asia from the engulfment otherwise facing it. I believe furthermore that we could do so with but a small part of our overall military potential committed to the purpose. There is no slightest doubt but that this action would at once release the pressure upon our forces in Korea, whereupon determination could be reached as to whether to maintain the fight in that area or to effect a strategic displacement of our forces with the view to strengthening our defense of the littoral island chain while continuing our naval and air pressure upon China's military potential. I am fully conscious of the fact that this course of action has been rejected in the past for fear of provoking China into a major effort, but we must now realistically recognize that China's commitment thereto has already been fully and unequivocally made and nothing we can do would further aggravate the situation as far as China is concerned.

Whether defending ourselves by way of military retaliation would bring in Soviet military intervention or not is a matter of speculation. I have always felt that a Soviet decision to precipitate a general war would depend solely upon its own estimate of relative strengths and capabilities with little regard to other factors. If we are forced to evacuate Korea without taking military measures against China proper as suggested in your message, it would have the most adverse effect upon the people of Asia, not excepting the Japanese, and a material reinforcement of the forces now in this theatre could be mandatory if we are to hold the littoral defense chain against determined assault. Moreover, it must be borne in mind that evacuation of our forces from Korea under any circumstances would at once release the bulk of the Chinese forces now absorbed by that campaign for action elsewhere—quite probably in areas of far greater importance than Korea itself.

I understand thoroughly the demand for European security and fully concur in doing everything possible in that sector, but not to the point of accepting defeat anywhere else—an acceptance which I am sure could not fail to insure later defeat in Europe itself. The use of force in the present emergency in the Far East could not in any way prejudice this basic concept. To the contrary, it would insure thoroughly

seasoned forces for later commitment in Europe synchronously with Europe's own development of military resources.

So far as your tactical estimate of the situation in Korea is concerned, under the conditions presently implied, namely—no reinforcements, continued restrictions upon Chinese Nationalist action, no military measures against China's military potential, and the concentration of Chinese military force solely upon the Korean sector, would seem to be sound.

I received this answer from the Joint Chiefs of Staff:

The retaliatory measures you suggest have been and continue to be given careful consideration. There is little possibility of policy change or other eventuality justifying strengthening of our effort in Korea. Blockade of China coast, if undertaken, must await either stabilization of our position in Korea or our evacuation from Korea. However, a naval blockade off the coast of China would require negotiations with the British in view of the extent of British trade with China through Hong Kong. Naval and air attacks on objectives in Communist China probably can be authorized only if the Chinese Communists attack United States forces outside of Korea and decision must await that eventuality. Favorable action cannot be taken on the proposal to obtain Korean reinforcements from the Chinese Nationalist garrison on Formosa, in view of the improbability of their decisive effect on the Korean outcome and their probable greater usefulness elsewhere.

In the light of the foregoing and after full consideration of all pertinent factors, defend in successive positions as required by the Joint Chiefs of Staff's message, inflicting maximum damage to hostile forces in Korea, subject to primary consideration of the safety of your troops and your basic mission of protecting Japan. Should it become evident in your judgment that evacuation is essential to avoid severe losses of men and materiel you will at that time withdraw from Korea to Japan.

I shot a query right back, asking for clarification in view of the self-evident fact that the strength of my command, as presently constituted, was insufficient to hold a position in Korea and simultaneously protect Japan against external assault. I suggested that strategic dispositions must be based upon an overriding political policy establishing the relativity of American interests in the Far East. There was no doubt but that a beachhead line could be held by our existing forces for a limited time, but this could not be accomplished without losses. Whether such losses were to be regarded as "severe" or not would to a certain extent depend upon the connotation one gives the term. After completing a long and difficult campaign, the troops were embittered by the shameful propaganda which had falsely condemned their courage and fighting quality. Their morale threatened to become a serious threat to their battle efficiency unless the political basis on which they were asked to trade life for time was quickly delineated, fully understood, and so impelling that the hazards of battle could be cheerfully accepted.

The issue really boiled down to the question of whether or not the United States intended to evacuate Korea, and involved a decision of highest national and international importance, far above the competence of a field commander guided largely by incidents affecting the tactical situation developing upon a very limited field of action. Nor was it a decision which should be left to the initiative of enemy action, which in effect would be the determining criterion under a reasonable interpretation of the Joint Chiefs' message. My query therefore amounted to this: was it the present objective of the United States political policy to maintain a military position in Korea indefinitely, for a limited time, or to minimize losses by the evacuation as soon as it could be accomplished?

I received no direct answer. A series of messages followed dealing with the details of a possible evacuation. Then on January 14th, I received a personal message from President Truman.

I wish in this telegram to let you have my views as to our basic national and international purposes in continuing the resistance to aggression in Korea. We need your judgment as to the maximum effort which could reasonably be expected from the United Nations forces under your command to support the resistance to aggression which we are trying to rapidly organize on a world-wide basis. This present telegram is not to be taken in any sense as a directive. Its purpose is to give you something of what is in our minds regarding the political factors. A successful resistance in Korea would serve the following important purposes: (a) to demonstrate that aggression will not be accepted by us or by the United Nations and to provide a rallying point around which the spirits and energies of the free world can be mobilized to meet the world-wide threat which the Soviet Union poses; (b) to deflate dangerously exaggerated political and military prestige of Communist China which now threatens to undermine the resistance of non-Communist Asia and to consolidate the hold of Communism on China itself; (c) to afford more time for and to give direct assistance to the organization of non-Communist resistance in Asia both outside and inside China; (d) to carry out our commitments of honor to the South Koreans and to demonstrate to the world that the friendship of the United States is of inestimable value in time of adversity; (e) to make possible a far more satisfactory peace settlement for Japan and to contribute greatly to the post-treaty security position of Japan in relation to the continent; (f) to lend resolution to many countries not only in Asia but also in Europe and the Middle East who are now living within the shadow of Communist power, and to let them know that they need not rush to terms with Communism on whatever terms they can get, meaning complete submission; (g) to inspire those who might be called upon to fight against great odds if subject to a sudden onslaught by the Soviet Union or by Communist China; (h) to lend urgency to the rapid buildup of the defenses of the Western world; (i) to bring the United Nations through its first great effort in collective security and to produce a free world coalition of incalculable value to the national security interests of the United States; (j) to alert the peoples behind the Iron Curtain that their masters are bent upon wars of aggression, and that this crime will be resisted by the free world.

Our course of action at this time should be such as to consolidate the great majority of the United Nations. This majority is not merely part of the organization, but is also the nations whom we would desperately need to count on as allies in the event the Soviet Union moves against us. We recognize, of course, that continued resistance might not be militarily possible with the limited forces with which you are being called upon to meet large Chinese armies. Further, in the present world situation, your forces must be preserved as an effective instrument, for the defense of Japan and elsewhere. However, some of the important purposes mentioned above might be supported, if you should think it practical and advisable, by continued resistance from off-shore islands of Korea, particularly Cheju-Do, if it becomes impracticable to hold an important position in Korea itself. In the worst case it would be important that, if we must withdraw from Korea, it be told to the world that that course was forced upon us by military necessity and that we shall not accept the result politically or militarily until the aggression has been rectified.

The entire nation is grateful for your splendid leadership in the difficult struggle in Korea, and for the superb performance of your forces under the most difficult circumstances.

I replied at once: "We will do our best." And I told my staff: "That, gentlemen, finally settles the question of whether or not we evacuate Korea. There will be no evacuation."

On January 22, 1951,

a mission headed by Ambassador John Foster Dulles came to Tokyo to work out final details of the peace treaty with Japan. They stayed until February 9th, and, with the complete co-operation of the Japanese, appeared to make firm progress. I worked hand-in-hand with Dulles, continually stressing the fact that Japan deserved the treaty and that its realization would restore a defeated people to their place among the nations of the world. The treaty itself would show the people of Asia that the United States was not a conqueror but a friend.

Not too long afterward, a peace treaty was signed in San Francisco amid great pomp and ceremony. I was not invited to attend. Perhaps someone just forgot to remember.

On December 23rd, General Walker was killed in a freak jeep accident. It was a great personal loss to me. It had been "Johnny" Walker who had held the line, with courage and brilliant generalship, at the very bottom of Korea, until we could save him by slicing behind the enemy's lines at Inchon. It had been Walker who, even in the darkest hours, had always radiated cheerful confidence and rugged determination.

It was a difficult time to change field commanders, but I acquired one of the best in General Matthew Ridgway. An experienced leader with aggressive and fighting qualities, he took command of the Eighth Army at its position near the 38th parallel. After inspecting his new command, he felt he could repulse any enemy attempt to dislodge it. On New Year's Day, however, the Reds launched a general offensive in tremendous force, making penetrations of up to 12 miles. It forced the Eighth Army into further withdrawal. By January 4th, the enemy had recaptured Seoul, and by January 7th, the Eighth Army had retired to new positions roughly 70 miles south of the 38th parallel.

The press of Europe and much of that of the United States cried hysterically that the United Nations forces "are going to be pushed into the sea"—a dire prediction that was solemnly repeated on the floor of Congress. But I figured it differently. The strategy of progressive weakness, because of stretched supply lines, was beginning to tell on the enemy, and disease was commencing to ravage his ranks. Typhoid fever and other widespread epidemics, which the Chinese did not know how to control, decimated their lines. At Ridgway's

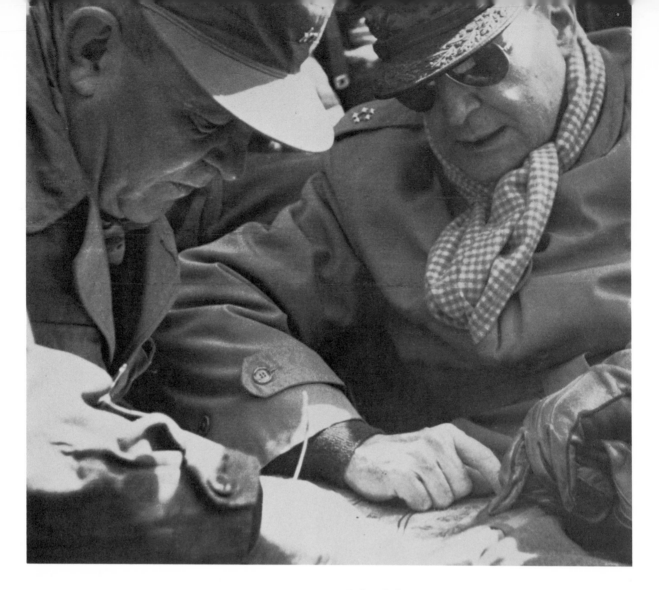

MacArthur at the front line
during U.N. offensive.
"There were but three possible courses:
I could go forward, remain immobile,
or withdraw. If I went forward
there was the chance that China
might not intervene in force
and the war would be over."

Below left:
Lieutenant General M. B. Ridgway, Commanding
General U.S. Eighth Army, greets MacArthur.

Below right: With Major General William Hoge.

headquarters, I told the correspondents:

There has been a lot of loose talk about the Chinese driving us into the sea, just as in the early days there was a lot of nonsense about the North Koreans driving us into the sea. No one is going to drive us into the sea. This command intends to maintain a military position in Korea just as long as Washington decides we should do so.

I ordered Ridgway to start north again. His first probing patrols struck in battalion strength. They met only light to moderate resistance, and the Eighth Army flowed forward. My plan was to push on until we reached the line where a balance of strength was achieved which was governed by the relativity of supply. I directed Ridgway: "Keep advancing until contact with the main line of resistance is established." By February 3rd, he had reached Haengsong, with the next stop the Han River just short of Seoul. By mid-February, I was able to report:

I am entirely satisfied with the situation at the front. The enemy has suffered a tactical reverse. His losses are amongst the bloodiest in modern times. He is finding it an entirely different problem fighting 350 miles from his base than when he had sanctuary in his immediate rear. He is paying now for the illusion so falsely but effectively propagandized that he had defeated the Eighth Army decisively. I note that Marshal Stalin has just predicted the annihilation of our forces in Korea—but his comrades will have to do lots better to prove him a prophet. Until I develop the enemy's main line of resistance, or the fact that there is no such line south of the 38th parallel, it is my purpose to continue ground advances. It is evident that the enemy has lost his chance for achieving a decisive military decision in Korea.

I now began to formulate long-range plans for destroying the Chinese forces in Korea. My decisive objective would be their supply lines. By constant, but ubiquitous ground thrusts at widely scattered points with limited objectives, I would regain the Seoul line for a base of future operations. I would then clear the enemy rear all across the top of North Korea by massive air attacks. If I were still not permitted to attack the massed enemy reinforcements across the Yalu, or to destroy its bridges, I would sever Korea from Manchuria by laying a field of radioactive wastes—the by-products of atomic manufacture—across all the major lines of enemy supply. The destruction in North Korea had left it bereft of supplies. Everything the Chinese used in the way of food or munitions had to come across the border. The

Reds had only ten days' supply of food in their North Korean dumps to feed nearly a million troops, and their ammunition was equally limited. Then, reinforced by Nationalist Chinese troops, if I were permitted to use them, and with American reinforcement on the way, I would make simultaneous amphibious and airborne landings at the upper end of both coasts of North Korea, and close a gigantic trap. The Chinese would soon starve or surrender. Without food and ammunition, they would become helpless. It would be something like Inchon, but on a much larger scale.

The first phase of this strategy went well. By the middle of March, we had retaken Seoul and reached the 38th parallel. The Joint Chiefs of Staff recommended to the Secretary of Defense that a naval blockade be imposed upon China, with the joint removal of restrictions on both air reconnaissance over China's coastal areas and those of Manchuria, and restrictions on Allied use of Chinese Nationalist forces. They also urged that logistic support be given to effectuate operations against the Communists.

General Ridgway wrote a strong personal note to General Collins, as one old friend to another, urging him to allow Chinese Nationalist troops to reinforce his Eighth Army. But, again, nothing was done. The Joint Chiefs of Staff's recommendation was turned down. And so was Ridway's personal request for Nationalist reinforcement.

The old debate whether or not the United Nations forces should cross the 38th parallel was again renewed. The scapegoat hunters, both abroad and in the United States, concentrated their fire upon me personally. Their propaganda charged that I had caused the Chinese Communists to enter the Korean War by arbitrarily crossing the 38th parallel. This was more than a mere rumor started by a few correspondents. It was a carefully outlined campaign exploited by anonymous sources high in governmental circles, and propagated by certain elements of the American press. The truth, of course, was that the decision to cross had been made in Washington.

The authorities made little effort to present the true and full picture of events in the Far East to the public. No information was taken from the dispatches recorded in these pages. Only information regarded as favorable to those in power was released. A muzzling order was issued that "no speech, press release, or other public statement concerning foreign policy or military policy will be released without clearance from the Department of the Army." I issued frequent communiques of the campaign and of the occupation of Japan, and sent the next one to Washington for clearance. It was returned to me stating it would not be necessary to clear such reports with Washington. The President confirmed this in a press interview in Florida.

On March 8th, Congressman Joe Martin, Minority Leader of the House of Representatives, wrote me as follows:

In the current discussions on foreign policy and overall strategy many of us have been distressed that although the European aspects have been heavily emphasized we have been without the views of yourself as Commander-in-Chief of the Far Eastern Command.

I think it is imperative to the security of our nation and for the safety of the world that policies of the United States embrace the broadest possible strategy and in our earnest desire to protect Europe we not weaken our position in Asia.

Enclosed is a copy of an address I delivered in Brooklyn, N. Y., February 12, stressing this vital point and suggesting that the forces of Generalissimo Chiang Kai-shek on Formosa might be employed in the opening of a second Asiatic front to relieve the pressure on our forces in Korea.

I have since repeated the essence of this thesis in other speeches and intend to do so again on March 28 when I will be on a radio hook-up.

I would deem it a great help if I could have your views on this point, either on a confidential basis or otherwise. Your admirers are legion and the respect you command is enormous. May success be yours in the gigantic undertaking which you direct.

I have always felt duty-bound to reply frankly to every Congressional inquiry into matters connected with my official responsibility. This has been a prescribed practice since the very beginning of our nation, and is now the law. Only in this way, and by personal appearance, can the country's lawmakers cope intelligently with national problems.

In due course, I replied to Congressman Martin on March 20th.

My views and recommendations, with respect to the situation created by Red Chinese entry into war against us in Korea, have been submitted to Washington in most complete detail. Generally these views are well known and clearly understood, as they follow the conventional pattern of meeting force with maximum counter-force as we have never failed to do in the past. Your view with respect to the utilization of the Chinese forces on Formosa is in conflict with neither logic nor this tradition. It seems strangely difficult for some to realize that here in Asia is where the Communist conspirators have elected to make their play for global conquest, and that we have joined the issue thus raised on the battlefield; that here we fight Europe's war with arms while the diplomats there still fight it with words; that if we lose the war to Communism in Asia the fall of Europe is inevitable; win it and Europe most probably would avoid war and yet preserve freedom. As you point out, we must win. There is no substitute for victory.

I attached little importance to the exchange of letters, which on my part was intended to be merely a polite response couched in such general terms as to convey only a normal patriotic desire for victory. My critics took particular exception to the statement that in war "there is no substitute for victory." The absurdity of such a complaint is apparent. As subsequent events so clearly demonstrated, the only substitute for victory lies in appeasement. A great nation which enters upon war and does not see it through to victory will ultimately suffer all the consequences of defeat. Stalemate may end the casualties on the battlefield, but marks the military collapse of the purpose which induced entry into combat.

On March 21st, I received the following message from the Joint Chiefs of Staff:

Presidential announcement planned by State shortly that, with the clearing bulk of South Korean aggressors, United Nations now preparing to discuss conditions of settlement in Korea. Strong United Nations feeling persists that further diplomatic efforts towards settlement should be made before any advance with forces north of the 38th parallel. Time will be required to determine diplomatic reaction and permit new negotiations that may develop. Recognizing that parallel has no military significance, State has asked Joint Chiefs of Staff what authority you should have to permit sufficient freedom of action for next few weeks to provide security United Nations forces and maintain contact with the enemy. Your recommendations desired.

I replied with an urgent request that "no further military restrictions be imposed upon the United Nations Command in Korea."

Before receiving this message, I had prepared the following routine communique to be issued from Tokyo as I left for the front:

Operations continuing according to schedule and plan. We have now substantially cleared South Korea of organized Communist forces. It is becoming increasingly evident that the heavy destruction along the enemy's lines of supply, caused by our round-the-

MacArthur presents award
of Distinguished Service Cross
to Master Sergeant Curtis D. Pugh
of Columbus, Georgia.

clock massive air and naval bombardment, has left his troops in the forward battle area deficient in requirements to sustain his operations. This weakness is being brilliantly exploited by our ground forces. The enemy's human wave tactics have definitely failed him as our own forces have become seasoned to this form of warfare; his tactics of infiltration are but contributing to his piecemeal losses, and he is showing less stamina than our own troops under the rigors of climate, terrain and battle.

Of even greater significance than our tactical successes has been the clear revelation that this new enemy, Red China, lacks the industrial capacity to adequately provide many critical items essential to the conduct of modern war. He lacks at this time the manufacturing and those raw materials needed to produce, maintain and operate even moderate air and naval power, and he cannot provide the essentials for successful ground operations, such as tanks, heavy artillery and other refinements science has introduced into the conduct of military campaigns. Formerly, his great numerical potential might well have filled this gap but with the development of existing methods of mass destruction, numbers alone do not offset the vulnerability inherent in such deficiencies. Control of the sea and the air, which in turn means control over supplies, communications and transportation, are no less essential and decisive now than in the past. When this control exists, as in our case, and is coupled with an inferiority of ground fire power as in the enemy's case, the resulting disparity is such that it cannot be overcome by bravery, however fanatical, or the most gross indifference to human loss.

These military weaknesses have been clearly and definitely revealed since Red China entered upon its undeclared war in Korea. Even under the inhibitions which now restrict the activity of the United Nations forces and the corresponding military advantages which accrue to Red China, it has shown its complete inability to accomplish by force of arms the conquest of Korea. The enemy, therefore, must by now be painfully aware that a decision of the United Nations to depart from its tolerant effort to contain the war to the area of Korea, through an expansion of our military operations to his coastal areas and interior bases, would doom Red China to the risk of imminent military collapse. These basic facts being established, there should be no insuperable difficulty in arriving at decisions on the Korean problem if the issues are resolved on their own merits, without being burdened by extraneous matters such as Formosa or China's seat in the United Nations.

The Korean nation and people, who have been so cruelly ravaged, must not be sacrificed. That is a paramount concern. Apart from the military area of the problem where issues are resolved in the course of combat, the fundamental questions continue to be political in nature and must find their answer in the diplomatic sphere. Within the area of my authority as the military commander, however, it should be needless to say that I stand ready at any time to confer in the field with the Commander-in-Chief of the enemy forces in the earnest effort to find any military means whereby realization of the political objectives of the United Nations in Korea, to which no nation may justly take exception, might be accomplished without further bloodshed.

On my return from the Korean battle front on the evening of March 24th, I made the following comments:

Everything goes well at the front. All elements of our forces are in fine spirit and fettle. The enemy supply lines are taking terrific punishment from our implacable air and naval bombardments, conducted under the field commands of General Partridge and Admiral Struble. There is no heavy ground fighting. Our troops maintain the initiative and the enemy continues to withdraw. South Korea is now substantially cleared of enemy forces and everywhere there is a quickening effort at rehabilitation and reconstruction. Seoul is beginning to resume some evidence of life. No further comment would seem to be necessary with reference to the 38th parallel, the status of which has been so thoroughly discussed in recent statements from Washington, London and other capitals. As a matter of fact it has never had any military significance. Our naval and air forces cross it at will and both ground forces have done so in the past.

While I did not know it at the time, this statement, addressed to my troops, to Korea, to Japan, and to the world at large, was to be my last as a commander.

A tirade of criticism was raised against my last communiques. The section that was seized upon was my offer to the enemy field commander to talk military terms. The argument was made that I had disrupted some magic formula for peace on which the United States had already secured international agreement and which it was about to announce. This was utter nonsense. No such plan was even in draft form. And what I said would entirely support any peace effort that might be made. Under any interpretation, it was only the local voice of a theater commander who carefully limited his own responsibilities by stating "the fundamental questions continue to be political in nature and must find their answer in the diplomatic sphere." Twice before, I had called upon the enemy commander to surrender and stop further

Facing page:
MacArthur arrives in Tokyo
after his dismissal
as Allied Supreme Commander.

bloodshed—after the Inchon victory and after our capture of Pyongyang. In neither instance had there been the slightest whisper of remonstrance from any source—indeed, quite the contrary. From the beginning of warfare, it has not only been a right, but a duty for a field commander to take any steps within his power to minimize bloodshed of the soldiers committed to his command. Complaint was made of my emphasizing China's weakness, but my statement was not only factual, but intended to present to the enemy the basic reasons why he should agree to stop the war. Actually, less than four months later the Russian initiation of a proposal for a conference to arrange an armistice was avidly accepted.

At this critical juncture, Congressman Martin, for some unexplained reason and without consulting me, released my letter. There was an instant hue and cry that I wanted to spread the war. This put the cart before the horse—I only wanted to end the war, not to spread it. I had not started it, and many times had stated, "Anyone in favor of sending American ground troops to fight on Chinese soil should have his head examined."

On April 11, 1951,

President Truman summoned the press to the White House and announced my relief from command in the Far East. His action was fraught with politics, as he was apparently of the belief that I was conspiring in some underhanded way with the Republican leaders. This was completely erroneous. I had no part whatsoever in the political situation. Although nominally Republican, probably because of my attraction to Abraham Lincoln, I had always expressed admiration for the basic accomplishments of the Democratic Party, and appreciation of its many great leaders. Such criticisms as I have made have never been of parties, but of what I regarded as concrete instances of mistakes and failures by the parties.

My relief was important, not because of the personalities involved, but as a symbol of a basic change in attitude toward Asia since our entrance into the Korean War. Of even greater significance were the calamitous events which resulted thereafter. A chain of reactions was set off which has prejudiced to its very foundation the struggle between the free and the Red world. The decision to meet Communist aggression in its military effort to seize Korea would have been a noble one, indeed, had it been implemented with unswerving courage and determination. But the United Nations proved unequal to the task. After Red China entered the conflict, it yielded to counsels of fear, and abandoned pledged commitments to restore to the people of Korea a nation which was unified and free.

Such abandonment of principles by the United Nations, in whose solemn declaration the peoples of Asia had placed such trust and faith, was a catastrophic blow to the hopes of the free world. Its disastrous consequences were reflected throughout Asia. Red China promptly was accepted as the military colossus of the East. Korea was left ravished and divided. Indo-china was partitioned by the sword. Tibet was taken almost on demand. Other Asian nations began to tremble toward neutralism. Sadly, we wasted the opportunity to retrieve the basic mistake of the 1946–1947 Marshall Mission in offering appeasement to the Red Chinese at the expense of Nationalist China, under the naive concept that the Reds were only agrarian reformers. It confirmed Red control of continental China, and fostered the growth of a powerful ally of Soviet Russia which well might become a balance of military power in the struggle for the world. It signalized the artificial restraint of our forces in Korea, which could have attained victory without recourse to other than conventional warfare and with much less than actually occurred under protracted negotiations. Approximately three-fifths of our casualties took place during the indecisive aftermath which followed my recall. It reversed United States military doctrine of a century and a half, from the attack to the defense, although the history of warfare shows the latter never attained more than an indecisive stalemate. It accepted at tragic cost the policy of indecision that in war there can be a substitute for victory; that enemy leaders who violate the conventional laws of warfare by savage brutalities need not be held to ultimate responsibility; that the rights of honorable prisoners of war are no longer a sacred national trust. All of this destroyed Oriental faith in Western fortitude, in Western determination, and in Western interest in Asia. This largely cost the free world its psychological gains which were the result of our World War II victory in the Far East.

There was an abysmal failure to comprehend the Soviet strategy in the latter's continuing and relentless effort to control the world, although that strategy is clearly expressed and delineated in the public writings of the Soviet leadership. There was a failure to understand that the global panorama has long encompassed three great areas of potential struggle: in the center, Europe; in the flanks, Asia to the north and Africa to the south. The free world apparently conceived of the center as the area of supreme interest and potential struggle; that if it could be held safely, all else would fall into place. This concept was fostered and encouraged by the constant propaganda pressures of the Soviet designed to convey the clear impression of aggression there and thus concealing his real objective to the flanks.

What the Soviets sought were the economic frontiers of the world, Asia to the north, Africa to the south—frontiers which possessed a mighty reservoir of the world's potential wealth in raw resources. The center represented little in economic advance, the flanks everything. The Soviet strategy was merely to defend in the center, but to advance by way of the flanks, to cause the free world to concentrate its resources at the center to the neglect of the vital ends. It has worked even beyond wildest expectations. The free world's main priority, even with war waging on the north flank in the Far East, has been the center; although practically free from battle combat, and now, with the north flank turned in Asia, the Soviet has started to envelop the southern flank. All this and more has followed from the United Nations' fatal decision not to see it through in Korea. The free world plunged from an invincible position of moral strength into the confusion of uncertain bewilderment. We fostered a practice of doubtful expediency and the eventual misery of timid appeasement. The result was a tragic and precipitous loss in prestige.

I was chided for regarding the Korean conflict as a war and not as a "police action." How could Red China have been more at war against us? Every ounce of her military and economic force was thrown into the Korean struggle. Lacking naval and air power, she was incapable of anything more. She was already strained to the breaking point, a 100 per cent war effort against us. How can one reasonably say it is not war when approximately 150,000 Americans and many times that of our ally, South Korea, were killed or maimed? The preponderance of these casualties were inflicted by Red China.

Attempts have been made to justify the extraordinary military policy which placed our arms in a straitjacket, based on the possibility that if we followed our tradition and fought to win, it might precipitate Soviet Russia's entry into the war. But the entry of Soviet Russia, or Red China, was a risk inherent in the original decision to intervene in Korea. At that time the possible consequences should have been weighed, and the decision taken with full acceptance of all the circumstances involved. Even had Russia desired to actively intervene, she would have found it militarily almost impossible to do so. Her position in Siberia was of necessity defensive and highly vulnerable because of her limited and tenuous supply line. This consisted of a single railroad system which could be cut by air interdiction almost at will. There was little local supply in eastern Siberia, and its military needs depended entirely upon this sole transportation system. At no place in the world would she have been weaker for battle. At this time, while we had the atomic bomb, she had not yet developed its manufacture. There was never serious danger of active Soviet intervention. The Russian policy is not to sacrifice its own troops, but to use those of its friends. The enormous expansion of Soviet influence since the end of World War II has been brought about without the Russian soldier firing a shot in battle. Basically, the problem was the indeterminate question of whether the Soviet contemplated the conquest of the world by military means or by more peaceful persuasion. If it intended to use force, the time and place would be at its own choice and initiative, and any action we might have taken to resolve the Korean situation could not have been a controlling factor in the precipitation of a world conflict.

Several years after my abrupt relief just when victory was within my grasp, the charge was made that I had been insubordinate. Nothing could have been more grotesque. It was completely repudiated by all members of the Joint Chiefs of Staff, my immediate military seniors in the conduct of the Korean War, who specifically denied under oath before the Senate Committee investigating the reasons for my recall, that I had ever committed such a breach of regulations. The committee itself was unanimous in its agreement. It was stated that General Bradley had charged me with such an offense. But General Bradley, in answer to direct questions by Senators George, Byrd, and Morse, three times swore that there had been no such dereliction on my part. Later, in an article carried in the *Saturday Evening Post*, Bradley went

so far as to say he thought that I *"might have been right"* in the Korean problem.

Field Marshal Lord Alanbrooke, the famous chairman of the British Chiefs of Staff, gave this estimate:

The decisions MacArthur finally arrived at as regards the war in Korea were, I think, based on a Pacific outlook and, as such, in my opinion were right. He has been accused of taking actions without previous political approval, but he had been unable to obtain the political policy and guidance he had sought. To my mind a general who is not prepared to assume some responsibility on his own, when unable to obtain political direction, is of little value.

And even President Truman's relief order contained this contradictory paragraph.

General MacArthur's place in history as one of our greatest commanders is fully established. The nation owes him a debt of gratitude for the distinguished and exceptional service which he has rendered his country in posts of great responsibility.

The legal authority of a President to relieve a field commander, irrespective of the wisdom or stupidity of the action, has never been questioned by anyone. The supremacy of the civil over the military is fundamental to the American system of government, and is wholeheartedly accepted by every officer and soldier in the military establishment. It was not an issue in this case. Since the beginning of time, commanders have been changed, some through whim, some through cause, but never in history was there a more drastic method employed than in my relief—without a hearing, without an opportunity for defense, with no consideration of the past. Up to the moment of my recall, I had been receiving laudatory commendations from the President, publicly and through his liaison officer at my headquarters. No slightest opportunity was given me to explain my position, to answer allegations or objections, to present my future concepts and plans.

The actual order I received was so drastic as to prevent the usual amenities incident to a transfer of command, and practically placed me under duress. No office boy, no charwoman, no servant of any sort would have been dismissed with such callous disregard for the ordinary decencies.

I was first appraised of the action through a press dispatch over the public radio. It is claimed that Washington tried to inform me, before announcing my relief to the public, through the

Secretary of the Army, Mr. Pace, then on a visit to Japan and Korea, but could not reach him. This is incredible. Secretary Pace had been with me in my office just before, and had reflected a most complimentary attitude in Washington. He was in Korea at the moment in immediate message contact with my headquarters, which had similar contact with Washington.

But if every allegation made by my detractors had been justified, they would all together have been but trivia compared with the great issues involved in the Far East. There could not have been a more distorted perspective, a more complete inability to put first things first.

The order for my relief reached Tokyo on the afternoon of the 11th as the radios broke through their normal programs to announce a special bulletin from Washington: "President Truman has just removed General MacArthur from his Far Eastern and Korean Commands and from the direction of the occupation of Japan." In the embassy we had just finished luncheon, and I was preparing to leave for the front in Korea. The bulletin had been heard by one of my faithful aides, Colonel Sidney Huff, who had been with me for many years. He informed my wife by telephone that I had been removed from command, with the only reason given a doubt that I would be able to "support the policies of the Administration." I saw the look of distress on her face as she told me, but as for myself I had long ago become shockproof. "Jeannie," I said, "we're going home at last." It had been a long tour— fifteen consecutive years of foreign service since I had left Washington to become military advisor to the Philippines.

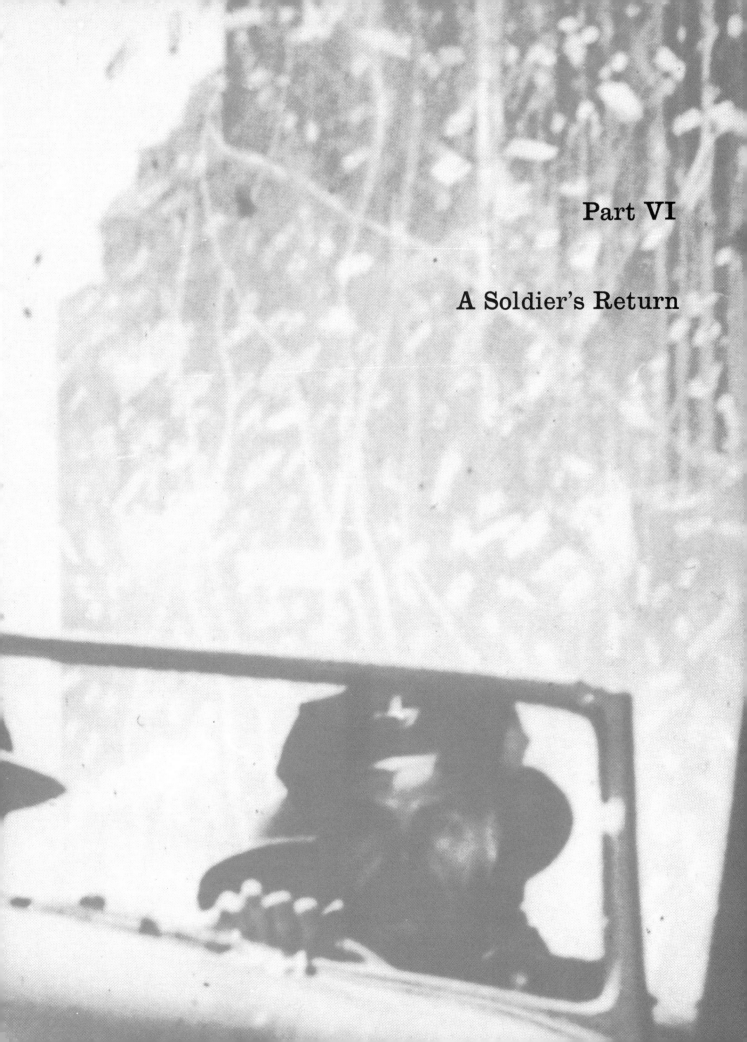

Part VI

A Soldier's Return

On April 16, 1952,

we left for Atsugi Airfield at daybreak. Two million Japanese lined the route from the embassy to Atsugi, waving and some weeping. All the dignitaries of Tokyo and its full garrison of troops were at the airfield. We took off as the sun rose with the breath of early spring in the air. Beneath us lay this land of the chrysanthemum, with its deep shadows and brilliant hues, with its majestic peaks and low-lying valleys, its winding streams and inland seas, its cities and towns and rolling plateaus. We circled Fuji for a last look and then we were gone.

But Japan did not forget. On the centennial of the first American-Japanese Treaty of Friendship, I was decorated with the Grand Cordon of the Order of the Rising Sun with Paulownia Flowers, one of the highest awards of the nation and reserved for monarchs and heads of government.

This honor moved me deeply, because I could recall no parallel in the history of the world when a great nation recently at war had so distinguished its former enemy commander. This feeling was intensified in that it came, not during my proconsulship, but only after time and thought, study and analysis had carefully evaluated the results of the occupation.

Our welcome home was tumultuous. It seemed to me that every man, woman, and child in San Francisco turned out to cheer us. I had been invited by Congress to address it at a joint session on the 19th, and flew on to Washington, where it looked as though the whole District of Columbia greeted our arrival. I mounted the rostrum and delivered the following speech.

Mr. President, Mr. Speaker, and distinguished Members of the Congress:

I stand on this rostrum with a sense of deep humility and great pride—humility in the wake of those great American architects of our history who have stood here before me, pride in the reflection that this forum of legislative debate represents human liberty in the purest form yet devised. Here are centered the hopes and aspirations and faith of the entire human race.

I do not stand here as advocate for any partisan cause, for the issues are fundamental and reach quite beyond the realm of partisan consideration. They must be resolved on the highest plane of national interest if our course is to prove sound and our future protected. I trust, therefore, that you will do me the justice of receiving that which I have to say as solely expressing the considered viewpoint of a fellow American. I address you with neither rancor nor bitterness in the fading twilight of life with but one purpose in mind—to serve my country.

The issues are global and so interlocked that to consider the problems of one sector, oblivious to those of another, is but to court disaster for the whole.

While Asia is commonly referred to as the gateway to Europe, it is no less true that Europe is the gateway to Asia, and the broad influence of the one cannot fail to have its impact upon the other.

There are those who claim our strength is inadequate to protect on both fronts—that we cannot divide our efforts. I can think of no greater expression of defeatism. If a potential enemy can divide his strength on two fronts, it is for us to counter his effort.

The Communist threat is a global one. Its successful advance in one sector threatens the destruction of every other sector. You cannot appease or otherwise surrender to Communism in Asia without simultaneously undermining our efforts to halt its advance in Europe.

Beyond pointing out these simple truisms, I shall confine my discussion to the general area of Asia. Before one may objectively assess the situation now existing there, he must comprehend something of Asia's past and the revolutionary changes which have marked her course up to the present. Long exploited by the so-called colonial powers, with little opportunity to achieve any degree of social justice, individual dignity, or a higher standard of life such as guided our own noble administration of the Philippines, the peoples of Asia found their opportunity in the war just past to throw off the shackles of colonialism and now see the dawn of new opportunity, a heretofore unfelt dignity and the self-respect of political freedom.

Mustering half of the earth's population and 60 per cent of its natural resources, these peoples are rapidly consolidating a new force, both moral and material, with which to raise the living standard and erect adaptations of the design of modern progress to their own distinct cultural environments. Whether one adheres to the concept of colonization or not, this is the direction of Asian progress and it may not be

stopped. It is a corollary to the shift of the world economic frontiers, as the whole epicenter of world affairs rotates back toward the area whence it started. In this situation it becomes vital that our country orient its policies in consonance with this basic evolutionary condition rather than pursue a course blind to the reality that the colonial era is now past and the Asian peoples covet the right to shape their own free destiny. What they seek now is friendly guidance, understanding, and support, not imperious direction; the dignity of equality, not the shame of subjugation. Their prewar standard of life, pitifully low, is infinitely lower now in the devastation left in war's wake. World ideologies play little part in Asian thinking and are little understood. What the peoples strive for is the opportunity for a little more food in their stomachs, a little better clothing on their backs, a little firmer roof over their heads, and the realization of the normal nationalist urge for political freedom. These political-social conditions have but an indirect bearing upon our own national security, but form a backdrop to contemporary planning which must be thoughtfully considered if we are to avoid the pitfalls of unrealism.

Of more direct and immediate bearing upon our national security are the changes wrought in the strategic potential of the Pacific Ocean in the course of the past war. Prior thereto, the western strategic frontier of the United States lay on the littoral line of the Americas with an exposed island salient extending out through Hawaii, Midway, and Guam to the Philippines. That salient proved not an outpost of strength but an avenue of weakness along which the enemy could and did attack. The Pacific was a potential area of advance for any predatory force intent upon striking at the bordering land areas.

All this was changed by our Pacific victory. Our strategic frontier then shifted to embrace the entire Pacific Ocean which became a vast moat to protect us as long as we hold it. Indeed, it acts as a protective shield for all of the Americas and all free lands of the Pacific Ocean area. We control it to the shores of Asia by a chain of islands extending in an arc from the Aleutians to the Marianas held by us and our free allies. From this island chain we can dominate with sea and air power every Asiatic port from Vladivostok to Singapore and prevent any hostile movement into the Pacific. Any predatory attack from Asia must be an amphibious effort. No amphibious force can be successful without control of the sea lanes and the air over those lanes in its avenue of advance. With naval and air supremacy and modest ground elements to defend bases, any major attack from continental Asia toward us or our friends of the Pacific would be doomed to failure. Under such conditions the Pacific no longer represents menacing avenues of approach for a prospective invader—it

MacArthur in the capital arriving April 19, 1951,
to address the Congress of the United States.

assumes instead the friendly aspect of a peaceful
lake. Our line of defense is a natural one and can be
maintained with a minimum of military effort and
expense. It envisions no attack against anyone nor
does it provide the bastions essential for offensive
operations, but properly maintained would be an invincible defense against aggression.

The holding of this littoral defense line in the
western Pacific is entirely dependent upon holding
all segments thereof, for any major breach of that
line by an unfriendly power would render vulnerable
to determined attack every other major segment.
This is a military estimate as to which I have yet to
find a military leader who will take exception. For
that reason I have strongly recommended in the past
as a matter of military urgency that under no circumstances must Formosa fall under Communist control. Such an eventuality would at once threaten the
freedom of the Philippines and the loss of Japan, and
might well force our western frontier back to the
coasts of California, Oregon and Washington.

To understand the changes which now appear
upon the Chinese mainland one must understand the
changes in Chinese character and culture over the
past fifty years. China up to fifty years ago was completely non-homogeneous, being compartmented into
groups divided against each other. The war-making
tendency was almost nonexistent, as they still followed the tenets of the Confucian ideal of pacifist

culture. At the turn of the century, under the regime
of Chan So Lin, efforts toward greater homogeneity
produced the start of a nationalist urge. This was
further and more successfully developed under the
leadership of Chiang Kai-shek, but has been brought
to its greatest fruition under the present regime, to
the point that it has now taken on the character of a
united nationalism of increasingly dominant aggressive tendencies. Through these past fifty years, the
Chinese people have thus become militarized in their
concepts and in their ideals. They now constitute
excellent soldiers with competent staffs and commanders. This has produced a new and dominant
power in Asia which for its own purposes is allied
with Soviet Russia, but which in its own concepts and
methods has become aggressively imperialistic with
a lust for expansion and increased power normal to
this type of imperialism. There is little of the ideological concept either one way or another in the Chinese makeup. The standard of living is so low and
the capital accumulation has been so thoroughly dissipated by war that the masses are desperate and
avid to follow any leadership which seems to promise
the alleviation of local stringencies. I have from the
beginning believed that the Chinese Communist's
support of the North Koreans was the dominant one.
Their interests are at present parallel to those of the
Soviet, but I believe that the aggressiveness recently

Above:
General MacArthur waves to his wife
while receiving the applause of Congress.

Below:
"Old soldiers never die;
they just fade away."

displayed not only in Korea, but also in Indo-China and Tibet, and pointing potentially toward the south reflects predominantly the same lust for the expansion of power which has animated every would-be conqueror since the beginning of time.

The Japanese people since the war have undergone the greatest reformation recorded in modern history. With a commendable will, eagerness to learn, and marked capacity to understand, they have, from the ashes left in war's wake, erected in Japan an edifice dedicated to the primacy of individual liberty and personal dignity, and in the ensuing process there has been created a truly representative government committed to the advance of political morality, freedom of economic enterprise, and social justice. Politically, economically and socially, Japan is now abreast of many free nations of the earth and will not again fail the universal trust. That it may be counted upon to wield a profoundly beneficial influence over the course of events in Asia is attested by the magnificent manner in which the Japanese people have met the recent challenge of war, unrest and confusion surrounding them from the outside, and checked Communism within their own frontiers without the slightest slackening in their forward progress. I sent all four of our occupation divisions to the Korean battlefront without the slightest qualms as to the effect of the resulting power vacuum upon Japan. The results fully justified my faith. I know of no nation more secure, orderly and industrious—nor in which higher hopes can be entertained for future constructive service in the advance of the human race.

Of our former ward, the Philippines, we can look forward in confidence that the existing unrest will be corrected and a strong and healthy nation will grow in the longer aftermath of war's terrible destructiveness. We must be patient and understanding and never fail them, as in our hour of need they did not fail us. A Christian nation, the Philippines stand as a mighty bulwark of Christianity in the Far East, and its capacity for high moral leadership in Asia is unlimited.

On Formosa, the Government of the Republic of China has had the opportunity to refute by action much of the malicious gossip which so undermined the strength of its leadership on the Chinese mainland. The Formosan people are receiving a just and enlightened administration with majority representation on the organs of government, and politically, economically and socially they appear to be advancing along sound and constructive lines.

With this brief insight into the surrounding areas I now turn to the Korean conflict. While I was not consulted prior to the President's decision to intervene in support of the Republic of Korea, that decision, from a military standpoint, proved a sound one, as we hurled back the invader and decimated his forces. Our victory was complete and our objectives within reach when Red China intervened with numerically superior ground forces. This created a new war and an entirely new situation—a situation not contemplated when our forces were committed against the North Korean invaders—a situation which called for new decisions in the diplomatic sphere to permit the realistic adjustment of military strategy. Such decisions have not been forthcoming.

While no man in his right mind would advocate sending our ground forces into continental China and such was never given a thought, the new situation did urgently demand a drastic revision of strategic planning if our political aim was to defeat this new enemy as we had defeated the old.

Apart from the military need as I saw it to neutralize the sanctuary protection given the enemy north of the Yalu, I felt that military necessity in the conduct of the war made mandatory:

1. The intensification of our economic blockade against China;

2. The imposition of a naval blockade against the China coast;

3. Removal of restrictions on air reconnaissance of China's coastal area and of Manchuria;

4. Removal of restrictions on the forces of the Republic of China on Formosa with logistic support to contribute to their effective operations against the common enemy.

For entertaining these views, all professionally designed to support our forces committed to Korea and bring hostilities to an end with the least possible delay and at a saving of countless American and Allied lives, I have been severely criticized in lay circles, principally abroad, despite my understanding that from a military standpoint the above views have been fully shared in the past by practically every military leader concerned with the Korean campaign, including our own Joint Chiefs of Staff.

I called for reinforcements, but was informed that reinforcements were not available. I made clear that if not permitted to destroy the enemy buildup bases north of the Yalu; if not permitted to utilize the friendly Chinese force of some 600,000 men on Formosa; if not permitted to blockade the China coast to prevent the Chinese Reds from getting succor from without; and if there were to be no hope of major reinforcements, the position of the command from the military standpoint forbade victory. We could hold in Korea by constant maneuver and at an approximate area where our supply line advantages were in balance with the supply line disadvantages of the enemy, but we could hope at best for only an indecisive campaign, with its terrible and constant attrition upon our forces if the enemy utilized his full military potential. I have constantly called for the new political decisions essential to a solution. Efforts have been made to distort my position. It has been said that I was in effect a war monger. Nothing could be further from the truth. I know war as few other men now living know it, and nothing to me is more revolting. I have long advocated its complete abolition as its very destructiveness on both friend and foe has rendered it useless as a means of settling international disputes. Indeed, on the 2nd of September 1945, just following the surrender of the Japanese nation on the battleship *Missouri*, I formally cautioned as follows: "Men since the beginning of time have sought peace. Various methods through the ages have been attempted to devise an international process to prevent or settle disputes between nations. From the very start, workable methods were found insofar as individual citizens were concerned; but the mechanics of an instrumentality of larger international scope have never been successful. Military alliances, balances of power, leagues of nations, all in turn failed, leaving the only path to be by way of the crucible of war. The utter destructiveness of war now blots out this alternative. We have had our last chance. If we will not devise some greater and more equitable system, Armageddon will be at the door. The problem basically is theological and involves a spiritual recrudescence and improvement of human character that will synchronize with our almost matchless advances in science, art, literature, and all material and cultural developments of the past 2,000 years. It must be of the spirit if we are to save the flesh."

But once war is forced upon us, there is no other alternative than to apply every available means to bring it to a swift end. War's very object is victory—not prolonged indecision. In war, indeed, there can be no substitute for victory.

There are some who for varying reasons would appease Red China. They are blind to history's clear lesson. For history teaches with unmistakable emphasis that appeasement but begets new and bloodier war. It points to no single instance where the end has justified that means—where appeasement has led to more than a sham peace. Like blackmail, it lays the basis for new and successively greater demands, until, as in blackmail, violence becomes the only alternative. Why, my soldiers asked of me, surrender military advantages to an enemy in the field? I could not answer. Some may say to avoid spread of the conflict into an all-out war with China; others, to avoid Soviet intervention. Neither explanation seems valid. For China is already engaging with the maximum power it can commit and the Soviet will not necessarily mesh its actions with our moves. Like a cobra, any new enemy will more likely strike whenever it feels that the relativity in military or other potential is in its favor on a world-wide basis.

The tragedy of Korea is further heightened by the fact that as military action is confined to its territorial limits, it condemns that nation, which it is our purpose to save, to suffer the devastating impact of full naval and air bombardment, while the enemy's sanctuaries are fully protected from such attack and devastation. Of the nations of the world, Korea alone, up to now, is the sole one which has risked its all against Communism. The magnificence of the courage and fortitude of the Korean people defies description. They have chosen to risk death rather than slavery. Their last words to me were, "Don't scuttle the Pacific."

I have just left your fighting sons in Korea. They have met all tests there and I can report to you without reservation they are splendid in every way. It was my constant effort to preserve them and end this savage conflict honorably and with the least loss of time and a minimum sacrifice of life. Its growing bloodshed has caused me the deepest anguish and anxiety. Those gallant men will remain often in my thoughts and in my prayers always.

I am closing my fifty-two years of military service. When I joined the Army even before the turn of the century, it was the fulfillment of all my boyish hopes and dreams. The world has turned over many times since I took the oath on the Plain at West Point, and the hopes and dreams have long since vanished. But I still remember the refrain of one of the most popular barrack ballads of that day which proclaimed most proudly that—

"Old soldiers never die, they just fade away."

And like the old soldier of that ballad, I now close my military career and just fade away—an old soldier who tried to do his duty as God gave him the light to see that duty.

Good-by.

My welcome throughout the entire land defies description. America took me to its heart with a roar that will never leave my ears. Everywhere it was the same—New York, Chicago, Boston, Cleveland, Detroit, Houston, San Antonio, Manchester, Fort Worth, Miami, Los Angeles, Little Rock, Seattle, Norfolk, Austin, Dallas, Portland, Murfreesboro, Honolulu, Milwaukee. Men, women, and children, rich and poor, black and white, of as many different origins as there are nations on the earth, with their tears and smiles, their cheers and handclaps, and, most of all, their heart-lifting cries of, "Welcome home, Mac." In New York, where I settled down to live, the crowd was estimated by city officials to be the largest up to that time. I found 20,000 telegrams and 150,000 letters waiting for me. They came from all over the world, from the high and mighty to the lowly and downtrodden. But of all those messages perhaps the one I most cherished was from my old chief, former President Herbert Hoover:

There is no way to measure the service General MacArthur has given the American people. He is the greatest general and one of the greatest statesmen of our nation's history. He is the greatest combination of statesman and military leader that America has produced since George Washington. It was his military genius which won the war with Japan. It was his statesmanship which turned away the natural enmity of the Japanese people. When at the time of the Japanese surrender, he marched his victorious men down the streets of Tokyo, the Japanese, breathing hate, turned their backs upon him. Six years later, when he went through the streets on his way home, the people bade him good-bye in tears. General MacArthur may say, "Old soldiers never die, they just fade away." Physically they will. But the great deeds of men live forever after them.

I was showered with countless awards and medals and decorations and made many speeches before state legislatures, universities, veterans organizations, civic bodies, and even the keynote address at the Republican National Convention in 1952. I found the liberties of private life refreshing and exhilarating. I entered the business world and became an executive of one of the larger manufacturing companies. I saw my boy graduate from Columbia University, and in peace and tranquillity I have enjoyed to the full the relaxation of release from the arduous responsibilities of high national command.

On December 5, 1952,

I made the following remarks on the Korean conflict at the annual dinner of the 57th Congress of American Industry, sponsored by the National Association of Manufacturers:

In Korea, the principle of collective security is now on trial. If it fails there—and thus far it shows few signs of success—it will fail everywhere. It is not the least of the strange anachronisms of these strange times that those who advocate most strongly the principle of collective security in the protection of Western Europe are either lukewarm or actually opposed to the successful application of the same principle in the protection of Korea and the Far East.

Indeed, if we would frankly face and review our own weaknesses we need go no further than the great tragedy of Korea. While it is well known that my own

views have not been sought in any way, yet I am confident that there is a clear and definite solution to the Korean conflict. There has been a material change in conditions from those of twenty months ago when I left the scene of action, and the solution then available and capable of success is not now entirely applicable. A present solution involves basic decisions which I recognize as improper for public disclosure or discussion, but which in my opinion can be executed without either an unduly heavy price in friendly casualties or any increased danger of provoking universal conflict. Until a solution is forthcoming, hundreds of thousands of the flower of American youth must continue their fight with only an occasional uneasy rest before re-entering the valley of the shadow of death.

So it has been these endless weeks and months which have grown into years since Red China initiated war against us in Korea and the indecision of our leaders committed us to the terrible blood tribute exacted by this type of stalemated attrition. Never before has this nation been engaged in mortal combat with a hostile power without military objective, without policy other than restrictions governing operations, or indeed without even formally recognizing a state of war.

Two days later, on December 7th, I received the following message from President-elect Eisenhower who was returning from an inspection trip to Korea:

Have just received aboard the *USS Helena* excerpts of your speech before NAM and am gratified by your continued interest in the Korean War which so vitally affects the United States and our Allies. Naturally I and my associates in the new administration, particularly the Secretaries of State and Defense, are vitally concerned about Korea and the Far East. We are now in the process of outlining a future program to be based upon the best interest of our country and the free world. It will aim, of course, at ultimate peace in that section of the world. I appreciate your announced readiness to discuss these matters with me and assure you that I am looking forward to informal meeting in which my associates and I may obtain the full benefits of your thinking and experience. With personal regards. Eisenhower.

I immediately replied as follows:

Dear Ike:
I have just received your message. I am grateful for your interest in my views concerning solution of the problems involved in the Korean War and the Far East. This is especially so because, despite my intimate personal and professional connection and well known concern therewith, this is the first time that the slightest official interest in my counsel has

been evidenced since my return. A failure of policy there might doom indefinitely the progress of civilization. A successful solution on the other hand might well become the key to peace in the world. You know, without my saying, that my service is, as it always has been, entirely at the disposition of our country. My best to you, Ike, as always.

MacArthur

On December 10, I received this message:

Thanks for your prompt answer to my cable. Because of persistent press speculation, I wonder if you would have any objection to my release of our two cables. Eisenhower.

I replied at once: "No objection whatsoever. MacArthur"

A meeting was held at the residence in New York City of Secretary of State designate John Foster Dulles on December 17. Those present were Eisenhower, Dulles and myself. In order that there be no misunderstanding or confusion as to my views and recommendations, I prepared and gave to Eisenhower a written memorandum reading as follows:

Memorandum on Ending the Korean War.

A successful solution of the problem of Korea involves political as well as military considerations. For the sacrifice leading to a military victory would be pointless did we not translate it promptly to the political advantage of peace. As a matter of historical record, the failure through inertia of our diplomacy to utilize the victory of Inchon and destruction of the North Korean Armies as the basis for swift and dynamic political action to restore peace and unity to Korea is one of the great contributing causes to the subsequent new war into which we were later plunged by Red China.

In April 1951, when I left the scene of action, the enemy, although well supplied with excellently trained infantry with adequate small arms and light equipment, had practically no supporting air power and was markedly deficient in artillery, anti-aircraft guns, transport and communications equipment. This permitted our own air to operate strategically and tactically with little or no opposition and made possible an early and inexpensive military victory through destruction of the enemy's bases of attack and supply north of the Yalu, conventional targets never before provided sanctuary in the history of war. Indeed, it is self-evident that the Red Chinese Commander would not have risked the entry of major forces into the Korean Peninsula without the knowledge previously gained, through indiscretion or leakage, of the extraordinary and unprecedented protection our military policy restrictions would afford

his supply lines and bases north of his point of entry which otherwise would have been at the complete mercy of our then largely unopposed air power.

Now after 20 months the situation as it then existed is markedly changed. The enemy reportedly has appreciable air forces with an arc of air bases extending from Port Arthur to Vladivostok to challenge our own air operations within the general area of the Yalu. He probably now has artillery superiority and through greatly increased motor equipment has largely solved the logistical problems which then confronted him. His communications now permit far more efficient tactical control of his front line units. But a change of even greater significance lies in the fact that through the ensuing 20 months the Korean war has grown to symbolize in the eyes of the world the struggle between the Soviet and the United States in which every facet of disagreement in every sector of the world is a part of the correlated whole. That this is so may well prove to our advantage if we utilize the fact with skill, courage and vision. For the capability which we still possess to destroy Red China's flimsy industrial base and sever her tenuous supply lines from the Soviet would deny her the resources to support modern war and sustain large military forces in the field. This in turn would greatly weaken the communist government of China and threaten the Soviet's present hold upon Asia. A warning of action of this sort provides the leverage to induce the Soviet to bring the Korean struggle to an end without further bloodshed. It would dread risking the eventuality of a Red China debacle and such a threat would consequently prove a powerful, possibly an all-powerful weapon in our hands.

To such end our consideration of the Korean problem should be broadened in the search for peace. A general outline of procedure might be as follows:

(a) Call a two-party conference between the President of the United States and Premier Stalin to be held at a mutually agreed upon neutral point. (The inclusion of the heads of other States would but enhance the possibility of disagreement and failure. Indeed, the President of the United States has every right to so confer on settlement of the Korean War by virtue of the designation of the United States as the agent of the United Nations in that conflict);

(b) That such a conference explore the world situation as a corollary to ending the Korean War;

(c) That we insist that Germany and Korea be permitted to unite under forms of government to be popularly determined upon;

(d) That thereafter we propose that the neutrality of Germany, Austria, Japan and Korea be guaranteed by the United States and the Soviet with all other nations invited to join in as co-guarantors;

(e) That we agree to the principle that in Europe all foreign troops should be removed from Germany

Above:
Washington, D.C.

Below:
New York.

Above left: Chicago.
Above right: Austin, Texas.

"America took me to its heart
with a roar that will
never leave my ears."

Below:
San Francisco.

and Austria, and in Asia from Japan and Korea;

(f) That we urge that the United States and the Soviet undertake to endeavor to have incorporated in their respective constitutions a provision outlawing war as an instrument of national policy, with all other nations invited to adopt similar moral limitations;

(g) That at such conference, the Soviet be informed that should an agreement not be reached, it would be our intention to clear North Korea of enemy forces. (This could be accomplished through the atomic bombing of enemy military concentrations and installations in North Korea and the sowing of fields of suitable radio-active materials, the by-product of atomic manufacture, to close major lines of enemy supply and communication leading south from the Yalu, with simultaneous amphibious landings on both coasts of North Korea);

(h) That the Soviet should be further informed that, in such eventuality, it would probably become necessary to neutralize Red China's capability to wage modern war. (This could be accomplished by the destruction of Red China's limited airfields and industrial and supply bases, the cutting of her tenuous supply lines from the Soviet and the landing of China's Nationalist forces in Manchuria near the mouth of the Yalu, with limited continuing logistical support until such time as the communist government of China has fallen. This concept would become the great bargaining lever to induce the Soviet to agree upon honorable conditions toward international accord. Should all efforts to arrive at a satisfactory agreement fail, then this phase of the plan should be considered in the light of conditions then existing).

It is obvious that American public opinion will not indefinitely countenance the present indecision and inertia. Underlying the whole problem is the indeterminate question as to whether the Soviet contemplates further military conquest or not. If it does, the time and place will be at its initiative and could not fail to be influenced by the fact that in the atomic area the lead of the United States is probably being diminished with the passage of time. So likewise is the great industrial potential of the United States as compared with that of the communist world. In short, it is not believed that any action we might take to resolve the Far Eastern problem now would in itself be a controlling factor in the precipitation of a world conflict. It is my own belief that the Soviet masses are just as eager for peace as are our own people. I believe they suffer the delusion that there are aggressive intentions against them on the part of the capitalistic world, and that they would welcome an imaginative approach which would allay this false impression. The Soviet is not blind to the dangers which actually confront it in the present situation, and it might well settle the Korean War on equitable terms such as those herein outlined, just as soon as it

realizes we have the will and the means to bring the present issues to a prompt and definite determination.

This memorandum is intended to present in broadest terms a general concept and outline without the encumbrance of detailed discussion. If its basis is acceptable, I shall be glad indeed to present my views as minutely as may be desired.

Douglas MacArthur

New York, New York
December 14, 1952

While Eisenhower was studying the memorandum I asked Dulles his own reaction. He said:

"Your premature relief has resulted tragically for the free world. I regard it as the greatest mistake Truman ever made. Your present plan is a bold and imaginative one and could well succeed. I believe, however, that Eisenhower should first consolidate his position as President before attempting so ambitious and comprehensive a program. It might take him a year to do so."

I replied that Eisenhower would be at the peak of his power and prestige the day he was sworn in as President; that every day after his inauguration his power with the people would diminish, the first three months arithmetically, the second three geometrically and the final six months astronomically; that by the end of a year he would be just the leader of his party fighting for the programs of his administration; that the plan represented action, to wait inaction; that he was the one American the Soviet esteemed highly; that if he did not act at once he could never do so, that it would then become too late.

On December 16 I received the following letter from the Chairman of the Joint Chiefs of Staff:

Dear General MacArthur:

The Joint Chiefs of Staff have discussed many possible courses of military action in Korea and we are interested in any new idea or suggestion that could possibly end this conflict on honorable terms acceptable to the people of this nation and to the United Nations.

We have been informed of your statement that there is a clear and definite solution which might end the Korean conflict. We would appreciate meeting with you at your earliest convenience to discuss this matter, or to receive your views on this matter by letter should it not be practicable for you to meet with us.

For the Joint Chiefs of Staff
Omar N. Bradley
General of the Army, Chairman

I replied at once:

December 16, 1952

Dear Mr. Chairman:

I have just received your note of the 16th and appreciate the invitation of the Joint Chiefs of Staff to confer with them on the Korean conflict.

I do have certain views concerning basic general policies differing materially from those now in effect, which I believe would produce favorable results. These views, however, involve predominant political decisions which are more vital than are the related military phases. To initiate implementation, action would require a longer period of time than is left to the present administration. This time factor makes it essential that the incoming administration make the fundamental decisions involved.

Prior to receipt of your note, I had accepted an invitation to confer on December 17 with the President-elect on the solution of the Korean problem. I am confident that he will bring to the attention of the Joint Chiefs of Staff anything suggested by me which he believes appropriately requires their consideration. If this necessitates a coordinated discussion of the matter with the Joint Chiefs of Staff, I should, of course be glad to participate. Any solution could hardly be of such military immediacy as could be reflected in an instantaneous cessation of daily casualties.

Very sincerely,
Douglas MacArthur

General Bradley replied on December 29:

Dear General MacArthur:

Thank you very much for your prompt reply to my recent letter. I have informed the Joint Chiefs of Staff of its contents and they appreciate, as I do, your position.

May I take this opportunity to wish you a happy and prosperous New Year. I hope it will find many good things coming your way.

With kindest personal regards.

Sincerely,
Omar N. Bradley

And from that day to this I have never been further approached on the matter from any source.

Great changes have taken place in our military establishment, some good, some not so good. Materially the improvement has been spectacular, psychologically yet to be proven. The men in the ranks are largely citizen soldiers, sailors or airmen—men from the farm, the city, from school, from the college campus—men not dedicated to the profession of arms; men not primarily skilled in the art of war; men most amazingly like the men you know and see and meet each day of your life.

Above:
Milwaukee.

New York.

Mrs. MacArthur during
the welcome-home parade
for her husband.

If hostilities come these men will know the endless tramp of marching feet, the incessant whine of sniper bullets, the ceaseless rustle of sputtering machine guns, the sinister wail of air combat, the deafening blast of crashing bombs, the stealthy stroke of hidden torpedoes, the amphibious lurch over perilous waves, the dark majesty of fighting ships, the mad din of battle and all the tense and ghastly horror and savage destruction of a stricken area of war.

These men will suffer hunger and thirst, broiling suns and frozen reaches, but they must go on and on and on when everything within them seems to stop and die. They will grow old in youth burned out in searing minutes, even though life owes them many tranquil years. In these troublesome times of confused and bewildered international sophistication, let no man misunderstand why they do that which they must do. These men will fight, and, perchance die, for one reason only—for their country—for America. No complex philosophies of world intrigue and conspiracy dominate their thoughts. No exploitation or extravagance of propaganda dims their sensibilities. Just the simple fact, their country called.

But now strange voices are heard across the land, decrying this old and proven concept of patriotism. Seductive murmurs are arising that it is now outmoded by some more comprehensive and all-embracing philosophy, that we are provincial and immature or reactionary and stupid when we idealize our own country; that there is a higher destiny for us under another and more general flag; that no longer when we send our sons and daughters to the battlefields must we see them through all the way to victory; that we can call upon them to fight and even to die in some half-hearted and indecisive war; that we can plunge them recklessly into war and then suddenly decide that it is a wrong war or in a wrong place or at a wrong time, or even that we can call it not a war at all by using some more euphemistic and gentler name; that we can treat them as expendable, although they are our own flesh and blood; that we, the strongest military nation in the world, have suddenly become dependent upon others for our security and even our welfare.

Listen not to these voices, be they from the one political party or from the other. Be they from the high and the mighty or the lowly and forgotten. Heed them not. Visit upon them a righteous scorn, born of the past sacrifices of your fighting sons and daughters. Repudiate them in the market

Above:
A portrait of West Point:
four of the Academy's superintendents.
(left to right) Generals Taylor,
MacArthur, Boyan, Davidson.

Facing page, top:
General and Mrs. MacArthur
visit Mary Martin backstage
at the Majestic Theater.

Facing page,
middle left:
MacArthur arrives
to take up residence
at the Waldorf-Astoria.

Facing page,
middle right:
Visit to West Point.

Facing page,
bottom left:
Wearing civilian clothes
for the first time in twelve years,
MacArthur waves to the crowd
at the Polo Grounds.

Bottom right:
New York. 1951.

Below:
Lunching with President-elect
Dwight D. Eisenhower after discussing
MacArthur's proposals
to end the Korean stalemate.

place, on platforms, from the pulpit. The highest encomium you can still receive is to be called a patriot, if it means you love your country above all else and will place your life, if need be, at the service of your Flag. Great changes, even more comprehensive than in the military field, have taken place in industry. In its massive and almost limitless potential, the rugged determination of its leaders, the skill and energy of its workers, there has been welded an industrial supremacy such as the world has never before known. It comprises not only a power in being but a reserve power capable of being quickly mounted to meet and overcome any eventuality that might arise. This not only insures a continuity of human progress but imposes an almost impassable barrier against any who would threaten the security of the American continent. It has thus become a leavening influence in a world where war and the threat and fear of war would otherwise so distort the minds of men as to threaten the progress of the human race.

It represents a condition of preparedness born of American enterprise and vision, nurtured upon American energy and incentive, and depending for its ultimate strength upon American will and determination. It is the result and fruition of the capitalistic system—a system embracing every segment of American society—the owners of industry, the workers in industry, the public served by industry. This free enterprise based upon the right to work and the right to possess the fruits of that work has created an economic freedom which is the basis of all other freedoms.

But this very success has created its own perils and harassments, both from without and within. For from one end of the world to the other there is a titanic struggle to seize control of industry and of the economics. Whether this be in the masquerade of Communism or Socialism or Fascism the purpose is the same—to destroy a primary element of Freedom and preempt it for the State.

The capitalistic system has hence become the great target, although it has never failed to provide the resource for an ever increasing standard for human life, has never failed to maximize the fruits of human energy and creative enterprise, has never failed to provide the sinews for victory in war. It has built this nation far beyond the wildest dreams of its architects; it has through the scientific advance of means of communication closed the international geographic gap to permit rapid and effective trade and commerce among

the peoples of the world, has elevated the laborer, the farmer and the tradesman to their rightful station of dignity and relative prosperity, and has established the pattern for modern industrialization and scientific development.

The first prominent opponent of capitalism was Karl Marx who shunned the use of violence and sought the voluntary acceptance of the principle of communal ownership of the sources and means of production. The innate common sense of the human race, however, rejected this principle and the element of force was injected by the Bolshevik after the close of the first World War. Then was combined the theory of Karl Marx with the principle of Nihilism under which the control of public policy was sought through terrorism and violence. This combination known as Communism has had many successes. The minority, the Communist Party, in many sectors of the globe has been able to establish its rule over the majority. Only where the concept of human liberty was most deeply rooted and greatly advanced were such minority pressures decisively thrown back.

Such was the case in this nation where our economy, built upon the principle of private capitalism, became recognized as the great barrier to the universal enforcement of the theories of modern Communism. There followed repeated and diversified efforts to reduce and destroy it. Resort was had to the control of private profit by the Marxism-inspired device of confiscatory taxation and the levies upon privately accumulated resources.

It began in this country with the Federal Income Tax Law of 1914 which gave unlimited access to the people's wealth, and the power for the first time to levy taxes not for revenue only but for social purposes. Since then the sphere of government has increased with a kind of explosive force.

Karl Marx, while planning the destruction of all constitutional government, said: "The surest way to overturn the social order is to debauch the currency." And the Russian dictator, Lenin, that implacable foe of the free enterprise system, predicted as early as 1920 that the United States would eventually spend itself into bankruptcy.

Karl Marx referred, of course, to the process of inflation, induced by extreme taxation; the process of "planned economy"; the process of controlling economic conditions and thereby controlling the lives of individuals—a control of fiscal, monetary and general economic forces which produce higher prices and a gradual devitalizing of the purchasing power of money. The continuing rise in the cost of living is due to our drift deeper and deeper into inflation until today our whole economic, social and political system is infected by an inflationary mentality. "Taxation, with its offspring inflation," said Lenin, in support of the basic thesis of Karl Marx, "is the vital weapon to displace the system of free enterprise."—the system on which our nation was founded—the system which has made us the most prosperous people of all history—the system which enabled us to produce over half of the world's goods with less than one-seventh of the world's area and population—the system which gave our people more liberty, privileges and opportunities than any other nation ever gave its people in the long history of the world. To destroy it is the sure road to Socialism. And by Socialism is meant the forcing of a centrally controlled economic life upon all persons in the nation under an authoritarian monopoly that is politically managed. Actually, there has been through the direction of our own public policy an incessant encroachment upon the capitalistic system. Most officials of our government over the past years will deny, and justifiably, any intent to establish in this nation the basis for the emergence of a Socialistic, much less a Communistic State, but the course of fiscal policy has done just that. The fact is unmistakeable and clear that if the capitalistic system—free enterprise—is to be preserved to the future generations of our people, the course of government must be oriented to foster and preserve adequate incentive to encourage the thrift, the industry and the adventure which brought our nation to its present pre-eminence among all of the other nations of the earth and which alone can carry it forward in peace and security and progress.

I realize full well that the restless spirit of the times seeks change. But change should not be made for the sake of change alone. It should be sought only to adapt time tested principles which have been proven in the crucible of human experience to the new requirements of an expanding society. To do otherwise is not true liberalism. The Constitution is not to be treated as an instrument of political expediency. Every move that is made to circumvent its spirit, every move that is made to over-centralize political power, every move that is made to curtail and suppress individual liberty is reaction in its most extreme form. For the framers of the Constitution were the most

Top: MacArthur, now a business executive, visits the Remington-Rand exhibit—New York.
Middle left: MacArthur celebrating his 80th birthday.

Middle right: President John F. Kennedy visits MacArthur to discuss problems in Asia.
Bottom: Visiting President Kennedy at the White House.

liberal thinkers of all the ages and the Charter they produced out of the liberal revolution of their time has never been and is not now surpassed in liberal thought.

The object and practice of liberty lies in the limitation of governmental power. Through the ages the constantly expanding grasp of government, which was infinitely the most difficult part Webster once said on the floor of the Senate:

"Our security is in our watchfulness of executive power. It was the Constitution of this department, which was infinitely the most difficult part in the great work of creating our present government; to give to the executive department such power as should make it useful, and yet not such as should render it dangerous; to make it efficient, independent and strong, and yet to prevent it from sweeping away everything by its union of military and civil authority, by the influence of patronage, and office, and force. . . . I do not wish to impair the power of the President as it stands written down in the Constitution. But, I will not blindly confide, where all experience admonishes me to be jealous; I will not trust executive power, vested in the hands of a single magistrate, to keep the vigils of liberty."

He spoke those words 129 years ago; but they could as well have been spoken but yesterday.

There are many who have lost faith in this early American ideal and believe in a form of socialistic, totalitarian rule, a sort of big brother deity to run our lives for us. They no longer believe that free men can successfully manage their own affairs. Their thesis is that a handful of men, centered in government, largely bureaucratic not elected, can utilize the proceeds of our toil and labor to greater advantage than those who create it. Nowhere in the history of the human race is there justification for this reckless faith in political power. It is the oldest, most reactionary of all forms of social organization. It was tried out in ancient Babylon, ancient Greece and ancient Rome; in Mussolini's Italy, in Hitler's Germany, and in all communist countries. Wherever and whenever it has been attempted, it has failed utterly to provide economic security, and has generally ended in national disaster. It embraces an essential idiocy, that individuals who, as private citizens, are not to manage the disposition of their own earnings, become in public office supermen who can manage the affairs of the world.

The fundamental and ultimate issue at stake is liberty, itself—liberty versus the creeping soci-

alization in every domestic field. Freedom to live under the minimum of restraint! A least common denominator of mediocrity against the proven progress of pioneering individualism! The free enterprise system or the cult of conformity! The result will determine the future of civilization. It will be felt on every human life. It will be etched in blazing rainbow colors on the very arch of the sky.

I made one further trip to the Far East, a sentimental journey to the Philippines as a guest of the nation on the fifteenth anniversary of its independence. I visited again the old historic spots—the white beaches of Leyte, the great central thoroughfare through Luzon, now named the MacArthur Highway, the rugged slopes of Corregidor gone back to jungle, the hills of Bataan under the shadows of the setting sun beyond Marivales. When last I had been there, the scene had been one of desolation and destruction. The war still raged. The crash of guns roared. The sputter of rifle fire filled the air. The acrid smell of smoke, the stench of death was everywhere. There was sorrow and bereavement in countless Philippine homes. Fire and sword had taken a toll of personal tragedy, searing the hearts and souls of every Filipino citizen.

But now their cities had been restored, their economy revived, their farm shortages turned into surpluses, their commerce expanded. Their products now reached the markets of the world. They had taken their place in the counsels of the nations with dignity and universal respect. All was light and laughter. And as I saw the happiness in their faces, as I saw the prosperity of the community, a great weight was lifted from my heart, and I thanked God that I was one of those who had helped them to freedom. Once again the fragrance of the ilang-ilang and the sampaguita filled the air as millions of devoted Filipinos greeted me with their welcoming shouts of "Mabuhay."

I tried to speak to them words of wisdom, but in my heart was only affection and remembrance.

I told them:

The tide of world affairs ebbs and flows in and out. Old empires die, new nations are born, alliances arise and vanish. But through all this confusion the mutual friendship of our two countries shines like a beacon in the night. Together we suffered in war. Together we seek the way of peace. And in this long twilight era, that is neither war nor peace, we stand as firmly as before, together.

Top: With Mr. and Mrs. John Glenn.

Left:
New York's Governor Nelson A. Rockefeller at
a luncheon celebrating the twelfth anniversary of
"Old soldiers never die" speech.

Bottom: MacArthur receives a new generation
of West Point cadets at his Waldorf apartment.
"The American man-at-arms is one of the world's
noblest figures. His name and fame are the birthright
of every American citizen. He belongs to history
as furnishing one of the greatest examples
of successful patriotism."

Top:
Reviewing troops at West Point for the last time.
Bottom left:
After delivering Sylvanus Thayer address—West Point.

Bottom center:
General and Mrs. MacArthur. 1962.
Bottom right:
Bust of MacArthur at West Point.

On May 12, 1962,

I was awarded the Sylvanus Thayer Medal, the highest honor of the United States Military Academy. That day, I reviewed the Corps of Cadets on the Plain at West Point, lunched with them at the mess hall, and then responded to the presentation. I had no prepared address, but my remarks were recorded as follows:

As I was leaving the hotel this morning, a doorman asked me, "Where are you headed for, General?" And when I replied, "West Point," he remarked, "Beautiful place. Have you ever been there before?"

No human being could fail to be deeply moved by such a tribute as this. Coming from a profession I have served so long, and a people I have loved so well, it fills me with an emotion I cannot express. But this award is not intended primarily to honor a personality, but to symbolize a great moral code—the code of conduct and chivalry of those who guard this beloved land of culture and ancient descent. That is the meaning of this medallion. For all eyes and for all time, it is an expression of the ethics of the American soldier. That I should be integrated in this way with so noble an ideal arouses a sense of pride and yet of humility which will be with me always. . . .

Duty–Honor–Country. Those three hallowed words reverently dictate what you ought to be, what you can be, what you will be. They are your rallying points; to build courage when courage seems to fail; to regain faith when there seems to be little cause for faith; to create hope when hope becomes forlorn. Unhappily, I possess neither that eloquence of diction, that poetry of imagination, nor that brilliance of metaphor to tell you all that they mean. The unbelievers will say they are but words, but a slogan, but a flamboyant phrase. Every pedant, every demagogue, every cynic, every hypocrite, every troublemaker, and, I am sorry to say, some others of an entirely different character, will try to downgrade them even to the extent of mockery and ridicule.

But these are some of the things they do. They build your basic character; they mold you for your future roles as custodians of the nation's defense; they make you strong enough to know when you are weak, and brave enough to face yourself when you are afraid. They teach you to be proud and unbending in honest failure, but humble and gentle in success, not to substitute words for actions, not to seek the path of comfort, but to face the stress and spur of difficulty and challenge; to learn to stand up in the storm but to have compassion on those who fail; to master yourself before you seek to master others; to have a heart that is clean, a goal that is high; to learn to laugh yet never forget how to weep; to reach into the future yet never neglect the past; to be serious yet never to take yourself too seriously; to be modest so that you will remember the simplicity of true greatness, the open mind of true wisdom, the meekness of true strength. They give you a temper of the will, a quality of the imagination, a vigor of the emotions, a freshness of the deep springs of life, a temperamental predominance of courage over timidity, an appetite for adventure over love of ease. They create in your heart the sense of wonder, the unfailing hope of what next, and the joy and inspiration of life. They teach you in this way to be an officer and a gentleman.

And what sort of soldiers are those you are to lead? Are they reliable, are they brave, are they capable of victory? Their story is known to all of you; it is the story of the American man-at-arms. My estimate of him was formed on the battlefield many years ago, and has never changed. I regarded him then as I regard him now—as one of the world's noblest figures, not only as one of the finest military characters, but also as one of the most stainless. His name and fame are the birthright of every American citizen. In his youth and strength, his love and loyalty, he gave all that mortality can give. He needs no eulogy from me or from any other man. He has written his own history and written it in red on his enemy's breast. But when I think of his patience under adversity, of his courage under fire, and of his modesty in victory, I am filled with an emotion of admiration I cannot put into words. He belongs to history as furnishing one of the greatest examples of successful patriotism; he belongs to posterity as the instructor of future generations in the principles of liberty and freedom; he belongs to the present, to us, by his virtues and by his achievements. In twenty campaigns, on a hundred battlefields, around a thousand campfires, I have witnessed that enduring fortitude, that patriotic self-abnegation, and that invincible determination which have carved his status in the hearts of his people. From one end of the world to the other he has drained deep the chalice of courage.

As I listened to those songs of the glee club, in memory's eye I could see those staggering columns of the First World War, bending under soggy packs, on many a weary march from dripping dusk to drizzling dawn, slogging ankle deep through the mire of shell-shocked roads, to form grimly for the attack, blue-lipped, covered with sludge and mud, chilled by the wind and rain, driving home to their objective, and, for many, to the judgment seat of God. I do not know the dignity of their birth but I do know the glory of their death. They died unquestioning, uncomplaining, with faith in their hearts, and on their lips the hope that we would go on to victory. Always for them—Duty–Honor–Country; always their blood and sweat and tears as we sought the way and the light and the truth.

And twenty years after, on the other side of the

Top left: "Today marks my final roll-call with you, but I want you to know that when I cross the river my last conscious thoughts will be of the corps—and the corps—and the corps. I bid you farewell."

Top right:
Douglas MacArthur II, Mrs. MacArthur, and Arthur MacArthur.
Bottom: New York.

globe, again the filth of murky foxholes, the stench of ghostly trenches, the slime of dripping dugouts; those broiling suns of relentless heat, those torrential rains of devastating storm, the loneliness and utter desolation of jungle trails, the bitterness of long separation from those they loved and cherished, the deadly pestilence of tropical disease, the horror of stricken areas of war; their resolute and determined defense, their swift and sure attack, their indomitable purpose, their complete and decisive victory—always victory—always through the bloody haze of their last reverberating shot, the vision of gaunt, ghastly men reverently following your password of Duty–Honor–Country.

The code which those words perpetrate embraces the highest moral laws and will stand the test of any ethics or philosophies ever promulgated for the uplift of mankind. Its requirements are for the things that are right, and its restraints are from the things that are wrong. The soldier, above all other men, is required to practice the greatest act of religious training—sacrifice. In battle and in the face of danger and death, he discloses those divine attributes which his Maker gave when He created man in His own image. No physical courage and no brute instinct can take the place of the Divine help which alone can sustain him. However horrible the incidents of war may be, the soldier who is called upon to offer and to give his life for his country is the noblest development of mankind.

You now face a new world—a world of change. The thrust into outer space of the satellites, spheres and missiles marked the beginning of another epoch in the long story of mankind—the chapter of the space age. In the five or more billions of years the scientists tell us it has taken to form the earth, in the three or more billion years of development of the human race, there has never been a greater, a more abrupt or staggering evolution. We deal now not with things of this world alone, but with the illimitable distances and as yet unfathomed mysteries of the universe. We are reaching out for a new and boundless frontier. We speak in strange terms: of harnessing the cosmic energy; of making winds and tides work for us; of creating unheard-of synthetic materials to supplement or even replace our old standard basics; of purifying sea water for our drink; of mining ocean floors for new fields of wealth and food; of disease preventatives to expand life into the hundreds of years; of controlling the weather for a more equitable distribution of heat and cold, of rain and shine, of space ships to the moon; of the primary target in war, no longer limited to the armed forces of an enemy, but instead to include his civil populations; of ultimate conflict between a united human race and the sinister forces of some other planetary galaxy; of such dreams

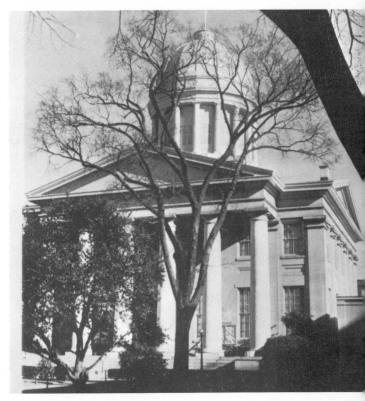

Above:
Starting the last journey.
Washington, D.C.

Facing page, top:
Washington.

Facing page, bottom:
President Lyndon B. Johnson
pays homage to a nation's hero.

Right:
The MacArthur Memorial
at Norfolk, Virginia.

and fantasies as to make life the most exciting of all time.

And through all this welter of change and development, your mission remains fixed, determined, inviolable—it is to win our wars. Everything else in your professional career is but a corollary to this vital dedication. All other public purposes, all other public projects, all other public needs, great or small, will find others for their accomplishment; but you are the ones who are trained to fight; yours is the profession of arms—the will to win, the sure knowledge that in war there is no substitute for victory; that if you lose, the nation will be destroyed; that the very obsession of your public service must be Duty–Honor–Country. Others will debate the controversial issues, national and international, which divide man's minds; but serene, calm, aloof, you stand as the nation's war guardian, as its lifeguard from the raging tides of international conflict; as its gladiator in the arena of battle. For a century and a half, you have defended, guarded, and protected its hallowed traditions of liberty and freedom, of right and justice. Let civilian voices argue the merits or demerits of our processes of government; whether our strength is being sapped by deficit financing, indulged in too long; by federal paternalism grown too mighty; by power groups grown too arrogant; by politics grown too corrupt; by crime grown too rampant; by morals grown too low; by taxes grown too high; by extremists grown too violent; whether our personal liberties are as thorough and complete as they should be. These great national problems are not for your professional participation or military solution. Your guidepost stands out like a tenfold beacon in the night—Duty–Honor–Country.

You are the leaven which binds together the entire fabric of our national system of defense. From your ranks come the great captains who hold the nation's destiny in their hands the moment the war tocsin sounds. The Long Gray Line has never failed us. Were you to do so, a million ghosts in olive drab, in brown khaki, in blue and gray, would rise from their white crosses thundering those magic words—Duty–Honor–Country.

This does not mean that you are war mongers. On the contrary, the soldier, above all other people, prays for peace, for he must suffer and bear the deepest wounds and scars of war. But always in our ears ring the ominous words of Plato, that wisest of all philosophers, "Only the dead have seen the end of war."

The shadows are lengthening for me. The twilight is here. My days of old have vanished tone and tint; they have gone glimmering through the dreams of things that were. Their memory is one of wondrous beauty, watered by tears, and coaxed and caressed by the smiles of yesterday. I listen vainly, but with thirsty ear, for the witching melody of faint bugles

blowing reveille, of far drums beating the long roll. In my dreams I hear again the crash of guns, the rattle of musketry, the strange mournful mutter of the battlefield. But in the evening of my memory, always I come back to West Point. Always there echoes and re-echoes in my ears—Duty–Honor–Country.

Today marks my final roll call with you. But I want you to know that when I cross the river my last conscious thoughts will be of the Corps—and the Corps—and the Corps.

I bid you farewell.